Synchronicity
The Entrepreneur's Edge

By

Jessika Satori, MBA, Ed.D

Boston Oxford Auckland Johannesburg Melbourne New Delhi

Butterworth-Heinemann supports the efforts of American Forests and the Global ReLeaf program in its campaign for the betterment of trees, forests, and our environment.

Library of Congress Cataloging-in-Publication Data

Satori, Jessika.
  Synchronicity : the entrepreneur's edge / by Jessika Satori.
    p. cm.
  Includes bibliographical references and index.
  ISBN 0–7506–9925–6 (alk. paper)
  1. Entrepreneurship—Case studies. 2. Coincidence—Case studies.
  I. Title.
  HB615.S312 1999
  658.4′21—dc21   98-32096
                                                                 CIP

British Library Cataloguing-in-Publication Data
A catalogue record for this book is available from the British Library.
The publisher offers special discounts on bulk orders of this book.
For information, please contact:
Manager of Special Sales
Butterworth–Heinemann
225 Wildwood Avenue
Woburn, MA 01801–2041
Tel: 781-904-2500
Fax: 781-904-2620
For information on all Butterworth–Heinemann publications available, contact our World Wide Web home page at: http://www.bh.com
10 9 8 7 6 5 4 3 2 1

Printed in the United States of America

To the One in all

Contents

Preface

If you doubt that synchronicity can occur, recall a time when circumstances happened to you in a coincidental way.

Have you ever decided to go to the store at an hour you wouldn't normally go, and met someone you needed to see there?

Have you searched to your wit's end to hire the right employee, and happen to sit next to a person at a dinner party who has the qualifications you are looking for?

Did you meet your life's partner or a business partner in a very unusual way?

These events are forms of synchronicity. Synchronicity has many faces and is known by different names: serendipity, coincidence, and chance are all related to this concept.

Recall the first time you heard the word synchronicity. Did you hear it as a part of the song of the same title by The Police? Perhaps you heard it as part of a conversation, or even have read Dr. Carl Jung's work on the subject. Jung also collaborated with physicist Wolfgang Pauli, and you may be more knowledgeable about Pauli's work. You may have read terms like "the square centimeter of chance" in Carlos Castenada's books, or Wordsworth's "spots in time."

Some people think of synchronicity as random occurrences, just something that happens to keep life interesting. But suppose that these events are meant to help us in decision making, to wake us up to an action that we may have not considered before. Maybe the outside world can reflect what is in the inner world of thoughts, intentions, and feelings.

Seattle's Mayor, Paul Schell, believed that one shouldn't underestimate the value of the chance encounter, and advocated the creation of city parks as a way to support the chance encounter that would lead to business creation, partnerships, and connections that would be of benefit to the community.

This book's purpose is to lead you in a discussion of synchronicity through the eyes of entrepreneurs. Many entrepreneurs are blessed by incidents of synchronicity that transform their lives and careers. This book will help you learn what synchronicity is, understand how it manifests itself in your day-to-day life, increase your awareness of it, and gain the benefits from it that others have gained.

MY JOURNEY

I was born on the cusp of the baby boom and generation X. I was not only between time, but I was between space. I grew up near the state line of two states in the Pacific Northwest.

Synchronicity is one of the ways I found to bring things together in space and time. It's the synthesis of intention in the inner world with creation in the physical world. Some would disagree about intention being an element, because intention is a conscious process, and in some ways it isn't even always conscious. Jung felt there were various ways intention worked, and outlined three ways; I proposed two ways as part of my study. Greg Steltenpohl of Odwalla, Inc. said they were "probably not the only ways in which synchronicity works."

Not only did the time I was born have an influence on my life, but a gathering of environmental or space/place factors had their effect; being born on the border of two states, for those who know, is like living with two sets of rules and values.

Like many entrepreneurs, I was born into a family of entrepreneurs and business owners and was encouraged in entrepreneurial ventures from the start. As a child I created puppet shows along with my siblings, doing everything from writing the script, making the puppets, advertising, to collecting admission, and performing customer service. In college I had a thriving alterations business, and later I freelanced in patternmaking and apparel design. All of these experiences laid the groundwork for business consulting later in life.

Three important experiences influenced me to consider synchronicity in my life. The first is my interest in interconnectivity—the belief that things are connected to each other, even though proof is vacant. The second is working with a prototype of a personal computer, and the third having experiences at work and in a community that supports thinking in a wider, more inclusive view.

First, I read things that made me wonder about highly achieving people and how they saw the world. I remember reading as a child about auto racing legend Jackie Stewart, how he felt when he drove his car. Before a race, he would imagine himself in his car, and all the space that surrounded his body be considered him as being a part of himself. The steering wheel was an extension of his body as was the seat and even the whole car.

Second, while quite young, I was exposed to what turned out to be a prototype of a personal computer. The machine itself was shaped like an old portable tape recorder, the size of a shoe box. Instead of a tape, you would put in a roll of paper, much like a player piano roll, only smaller and with text instead of music. I wondered, even at five, what use this machine would have later in my life.

Third, I can reflect on my unusual work life in view of the different "ages": agrarian, industrial, and informational. I experienced the agrarian age growing up on a farm, the industrial age in the years I participated in the apparel industry, and the informational age when I pointed my vocation in the direction of consulting.

As an entrepreneur, synchronicity was a factor in various consulting experiences. I am an experienced consultant for records, information, and archives with my business For The Record; for graduate students with my business Dissertation Consult; for personal development in my businesses Fireflight and Your Next Step. All of these businesses depended on my awareness of synchronicity as a part of the creation and maintenance cycles of businesses. The publication of this book was a result of a series of events that could only be called synchronistic.

I began to wonder if other entrepreneurs had the same experiences. I collected these stories over many years, and as a part of a dissertation, analyzed them and tried to understand what makes these events happen. How can they be explained? Do they happen to everyone? Do they occur more in a crisis or need-to-know situation?

I started to notice these stories in books and magazines. The more I spoke with the entrepreneurs, the more they acknowledged this phenomenon. One example is from the *Soul of Business,* by Tom's of Maine co-founder, Tom Chappell:

> I invited Father Allen to join the board [of directors]. He said he'd think about it, though he warned me that his church duties and his Native American concerns did not leave him much time. Back in Maine, I mailed him a formal invitation. Over the next few weeks we tried to reach him by phone to get his answer, without any luck. One day, waiting for a plane at New York's La Guardia Airport, I decided to call Father Allen one more time. I looked for a phone and saw the same Father Allen sitting across the lobby, waiting for a plane to Minneapolis. He was just as surprised to see me as I was to see him. I asked him if he'd made up his mind. "I've been waiting for a sign to help me make a decision," he said. "Seeing you here is more than enough. I would love to be on your board, if you still want me."[1]

1. Tom Chappell, *The Soul of Business* (New York: Bantam, 1993) 102.

BEING ON THE EDGE

I have been aware of and have recorded synchronistic events throughout my life, and I have noticed them in the workplace when working for others. The frequency of these events increased when I began my own companies and adopted leadership roles in my community. People ask "What is it like, being out on a limb, on the edge—never knowing when your next client or check may be coming?" But the clients came, and when I would end a consulting period on a Friday, I would have a client to go to on Monday. Synchronicity manifested in other ways, too. For example, I would bring in a seemingly unrelated book on a certain day and it would be just what the client needed to solve a problem on that particular day. I believe there is a great story to be told here, and it is one of my life's purposes to bring it to a larger audience to assist people in making decisions for the common good by being aware of synchronicity.

"On the edge" can denote an idea of being on the mental edge: sharp, quick, powerful; the awareness to recognize the cutting edge: the new, the creative; and the ability to face the unknown while standing on the edge of the known. It can also mean the edge of perfection, the ability to develop uncommon ideas that determine new products and services. Too extreme is "over the edge" or "being edgy" and can mean instability, irritability, or being mentally overextended. It can also mean you could be pushed over the edge, or you could be cut by being on the edge.

Benefits you will gain by reading this book include understanding what synchronicity is, discovering how it applies to making decisions for business creation (it could be considered a "consciousness" feasibility plan), and seeing how this phenomenon has played itself out in other situations.

This book is intended for a business audience and is written in a straightforward, action-oriented style, including examples that are relevant for business situations or to the inner thoughts of business people. This book's contents include definitions, discussions, and exercises. All of the stories are directly attributed to the participants; if they did not wish to be identified, their names were not included or a pseudonym was used. All stories are exact or based directly on experiences that happened in real life.

This book is divided into four parts. I've chosen the metaphor of the elements of earth, air, fire, and water. All of these elements have meaning when we consider that synchronicity seems to be like the alchemists of old. They mixed elements together to form different products, precious things on the way to their ultimate goal of gold. We are mixing the elements not only of earth, air, fire, and water, but the elements of synchronicity that result in our treasure, our gold.

PART I: EARTH

Building: The Foundation of Synchronicity In this segment, we will start on the ground level to build a foundation of synchronicity. We'll explore together how the concept of synchronicity developed as a part of the study of physics and psychology; how it affects our lives; and then look at and discuss entrepreneurs' stories of synchronicity and how they started their businesses. From there, we'll uncover the entrepreneurial mindset, how entrepreneurs perceive the world differently from people who are not entrepreneurs.

PART II: FIRE

Action: Developing Synchronicity Skills To me, fire denotes action. This section of the book will outline six characteristics that entrepreneurs possess, that help them to be aware of and use synchronicity as a part of their business life. The six areas will be packed with stories from entrepreneurs, examples from my consulting practice, and will include quotes from wise sages. We'll look at creativity, optimism, and goal setting as a crucial part of developing a direction for the company, then

discuss being open to situations and opportunities that may be sparks of synchronicity. Working with risk and interconnectivity are areas that will close this part of the book. Most importantly, at the end of each chapter you will find exercises to strengthen your awareness of synchronicity and give you practical application in your entrepreneurial life.

PART III: WATER

Reflection: Depth Dimensions of Synchronicity

Water is reflective (no pun intended). This part includes chapters on barriers and ethics. The barriers chapter examines reasons why synchronicity is still seen as something strange and not given credence in life, let alone the workplace. This is a chapter where skeptics can find solace in understanding these events. I will take you step by step through different questions about synchronicity, questions that discuss fear, empirical evidence, and the age-old question, "Why can't it appear when I want it?" The chapter on ethics—If I Don't Do it, Somebody Else Will and They'll Make Money: Toward a Synchronicity Ethic—will challenge you to think of the ways that synchronicity, as a gift, can be used for good or for evil. We talk about the filters we look through, some that can strain the impurities, others that can make us unaware of what effect we have on others, and what is going on in the "outside world."

PART IV: AIR

Regeneration: How Can My New Awareness Help Me Recreate My Life?

This part is also divided into two chapters. The first focus is on vocation, where we'll take a look at synchronistic events and how they have influenced our lives, especially the choices we've made in our vocation, our careers, and work life.

The second chapter—The Case for Grace: The Spiritual Aspects of Synchronicity—looks at how synchronicity has influenced and does influence the way we look at our inter-action with God, or whomever we consider our spiritual source.

AT THE CROSSROADS: SYNCHRONICITY DIAGRAM

Kammerer, an Austrian biologist who lived at the turn of the 20th century, called synchronicity "the umbilical cord that connects thought, feelings, science, and art with the womb of the universe which gave birth to them."[2] It would be helpful to have a diagram to understand all of these components in a business context.

Synchronicity connects at the crossroads of time and space, the inner world of the entrepreneur—feeling, faith, emotions,

2. David Peat, *Synchronicity: The Bridge Between Matter and Mind* (New York: Bantam, 1987) 9.

passions, and intention combining with the outer world competencies of operating a business: research and development, marketing, managing, accounting, and evaluation. Spirituality encircles the diagram, making a wheel of motion.

This book will focus mainly on the three highlighted areas: the inner world of the entrepreneur, synchronicity, and spirituality. My hope is that you will be able to see how synchronicity plays a role in your life; how the intersections in your life are brought together by these occurrences, parts of your life that you never considered joined before: your worklife with your spiritual life, your work as a leader with your home life, your past experience with your future potential. Synchronicity combines them all, setting them all into action.

My hope is that you take what you learn here and put it into action, that is, become more aware of synchronicity in your business and other lives. It has made a big difference in my life and the lives of the entrepreneurs with whom I've talked. We are all looking for answers about our lives in new ways, and synchronicity can be one of our tools to find these answers.

Pierre Teilhard de Chardin once wrote, "A new domain of psychical expansion, that is what we lack. And it is staring us in the face if we would only raise our heads to look at it . . ."[3]

---

3. Pierre Teilhard de Chardin, *The Phenomenon of Man* (New York: Harper & Row, 1959) 253.

Acknowledgments

No person completes the book process alone. The confluences of energies include three very special people who made this book a reality.

A big thank you goes to Barbara Shipka, whom I consider to be a Beryl Markham of current time. I admire her tenacity and courage. Barbara, because of her openness to synchronicity, was instrumental in leading me to Karen Speerstra, publishing director for Butterworth-Heinemann. Karen, I see as Hildegard of Bingen, successfully keeping all roles that she plays in place, all the while being highly creative.

It was because of Karen's wisdom and determination that this book has found a voice on the printed page. I am grateful. It was also because of Karen that I had the opportunity to work with Rita Lombard. If Barbara is Beryl, and Karen is Hildegard, I think of Rita as Bridgit. I know of two Bridgits in history: one Bridgit was the leader of an abbey in Kildare, and the other legendary Bridgit was a midwife. I have Rita to thank for coaching me through the stages of labor with this manuscript, keeping our senses of humor while keeping on track. Thank you for helping my writing be more concise and to the point.

Various entrepreneurs have inspired me in many ways, one of which is their daily decision to balance their principles with the profits of their companies. All of the entrepreneurs who participated in the survey or interviews are especially given thanks for making time to assist me. I thank many others who shared their stories and those who lead me to the entrepreneurs: Alan Reder, Marie Morgan, Mark Albion, Rinaldo Brutico, Mary Scott, Ken Willig, John Renesch, Alisa Gravitz, Jennifer Chapman, Dennis Macray, Steve Sunde, Claire Wehrley. And a very special thank you to Willis Harman.

Readers included Marj Watkins, Terry Persun, Dave Potter, Jennifer Rich, Dennis Roberts, and Irene Hays. Thank you for your time and energy to make this document sparkle.

People who either helped me directly or have been an inspiration to me include Barbara Marx Hubbard, Nancy Carroll, Anna Lemkov, Donna Copeland, Mary Stewart Hall, Bill Kautz, Charles Simonyi, Mary Kay Ash, Willis Harman, Jeffrey Mishlove, Roger Frantz, Alan Reder, Larry Dossey, Margo Keller, Susan Montoya, Ken and Noreen Willig, Patricia Weenolsen, Brian Cordell, Pat Logie, Kathy Pieples, Sally Branagan, and Sherri Stemp. Thanks to Dan Keursal for the Jungian understanding and the "Field of Dreams." Thanks too for the inspiration of the "three graces": Blanche Caffiere, Joyce Delbridge, and Virginia Dodge Harding. I would also like to thank Carter Castle and Debra Vaughn, Jan Perry, Danny O'Keefe, Erica Helm Meade, Janice Randall, The Port Townsend Writer's Conference with instructors Bill Kittridge and Annick Smith. And special thanks to John Schaeffer.

To all the librarians and library staff who are the caretakers of the internally managed forests, the libraries and archives from which I was able to extract information in a short amount of time. Special thanks to Sue Terrible of the Microsoft Archives.

My thanks to my parents and to my siblings and their families, for their continued support and for travelling the many roads with me.

Thanks to the natural world: to nature in all her forms for sustaining me always, but especially in the writing of this book, and for providing the means that conveys these words to the reader.

There were certain people who did not wish to be a part of this acknowledgement by name, but whom I would like to thank with all my heart. You made it possible for me to complete this book, to bring it to a larger audience.

I also want to thank special people who have played important roles in my life—Rev. Dr. John Neal, Rev. Susan Creighton, Rev. Linda Spencer, and Penny Herman—and to the spiritual communities, especially Lectio Divina, that have supported me in many ways throughout my journey.

To the One that leads me to the rock that is higher than I.

Part I

Earth
The Foundation of Synchronicity

In this segment, we will start on the ground level to build a foundation of synchronicity.

To put yourself in a frame of mind to read this section, consider the following questions and comments.

- When I stand on the ground floor, what do I see?
- When first learning about a new concept, what do I compare it to?
- Does synchronicity already happen in your life? Have I felt the "hand" of synchronicity playing in your life?
- What questions do I have?
- What doubts do I have?
- How can I understand this concept better?
- How does it affect entrepreneurs?
- How does it affect me?

Chapter 1

Synchronicity
Random or Intentional Events?

Imagine that you and your business partner have been creating a business plan, one to launch a publication of your own creation, design, and passion. You and your partner come up with a marketing plan that will cost $14,500 to launch. The problem is, neither one of you has that amount of money. You and your partner decide you both want to think about it a few days before asking other people. But the both of you still have faith in your plan to create the publication.

You go home and your brother calls. "Did you get your check?"

"What check?" you respond.

"Your inheritance check."

You walk over to the pile of mail and open the envelope and there staring back at you is a check for $14,500.

This incident, told to me by Marjorie Kelly, founder of *Business Ethics* magazine, illustrates what is known as *synchronicity*. The purpose of this book is to explore how synchronicity occurs as a legitimate and valid part of business development. It seeks to establish the connections between the Jungian concept of time-space relations and how today's business leaders and entrepreneurs can be aware of synchronistic situations to use them ethically in the workplace. Research that I have performed as a part of a doctorate study has shown that 86 percent of entrepreneurs believe that synchronicity has influenced their decision making and many say the phenomenon continues to guide their business decision making. This study included 28 entrepreneurs from different facets of business: high tech, food processing, retail, and restaurants. Demographically, they were from 11 states, and one was from Brazil.

What is synchronicity? Is it something only a few of us experience, or is it much more common than we suppose? What about those who dismiss it as blind luck? a hoax? something that is interesting when it happens, but has nothing to do with everyday life? Others may think that business success is only due to hard work and good marketing, or a formula of luck + opportunity = success. What makes it worthy of being taken seriously? The business entrepreneurs I talked with attest to the great value of synchronicity. Even entrepreneurs who were not part of the study are familiar with the sayings "timing is everything" or "being in the right place at the right time." Even business journals and magazines have eye-catching ads that include the phrase "timing is everything." If time and place are so crucial to the success of a business, how can we understand synchronicity as a benefit for us? Is there a way we can make it occur in our lives more often?

Initially, it's helpful to start putting synchronicity into a context, thereby coming to a comprehensive and understandable working definition of synchronicity. Dr. Carl Jung, credited with coining the concept, wrote that *synchronicity was the meaningful coincidence between an inner psychic state and an outward physical manifestation or event*. There are four key words and phrases in his definition. We'll take the last two concepts first, "inner psychic state" and the "outward physical manifestation." This explanation centers on two ingredients to create a synchronistic moment—internal variables (how an individual is feeling, his or her inner/psychological state) and external events or happenings (what's going on outside of the individual, how the feelings and internal variables show themselves). The two work in a meaningful concordance of sorts, the conjunction and coalescence of which cannot be explained by anything other than synchronicity. Something meaningful is personal in nature; it denotes that something happening outside resonates with something already inside of us, something deeply important. It catches our attention, holds us captive. Coincidence is an event that comes together in time and space, that seems so beyond probability that it is amazing, and we can shake our heads in wonder.

Time and space are fundamental to our reaching an understanding of the synchronistic phenomenon. Time (linear and chronological time) has only been measured for approximately the last 500 years by timepieces. Before that, time was measured by tides (where the word *time* came from), phases of the moon and the sun, and the seasons. A helpful way to explore the dual yet interchangeable concepts of time and space is to examine two words the Greeks have for time: *chronos* and *kairos*.

DEFINITIONS OF TIME:
CHRONOS AND KAIROS

Chronos (sometimes spelled *Kronos*), after the Greek god of time, refers to the measure of time. It's the origin of the word chronology. It is linear time, the time found in our appointment books, our watches, city clocks. Chronos is present in archives, libraries, museums, cemeteries; at meetings and appointments, at games and sports competitions; in strategic planning sessions and in planning annual meetings.

Kairos, on the other hand, is time that works in a different manner than chronological time; it is the time we sense when we are not being driven by a clock. These can be instances of "flow" when time seems to go incredibly quickly, as in a meeting with an interesting person. You and this person are so caught up in the exchange that you look at your watch and it is an hour later than you thought.

Madeline L'Engle, in *A Circle of Quiet*, compares the two times:

> Chronology, the time which changes things, makes them grow older, wears them out, and manages to dispose of them, chronologically, forever. Thank God there is Kairos, too: again the Greeks were wiser than we are. They had two words for time: Chronos and Kairos.
>
> Kairos is not measurable. Kairos is ontological. In kairos we *are*, we are fully in *isness*, not negatively, as Sartre saw the isness of the oak tree, but fully, wholly, positively. Kairos can sometimes enter, penetrate, break through chronos; the child at play, the painter at his easel, Serkin playing the *Appassionata*, are in kairos. The saint at prayer, friends around the dinner table, the mother reaching out her arms for her newborn baby, are in kairos.[1]

There are times in our lives that both kairos and chronos are important for balance in our everyday life. It seems that most of us live on chronos as if it were a planet, enslaved by the idea that our value and worth as people have to do with our effective use of time. Did we get the project done on time? When do the kids need to be picked up? Will I get to the airport on time?

Kairos is what we need to allow into our lives, too—and it has its own rules. It's a feeling of letting go of the control of time, of what has to happen in a certain length of time, or the required outcome. This kind of time refills us and inspires us.

There are intersections in kairos and chronos time. This is when synchronicity can occur. We are in our busy chronos lives, going about our day, and suddenly something hits us; it may be a comment, an article, a letter. Suddenly, we can find ourselves transformed by an event that puts us into the uncontrolled kairos time. Synchronicity can be like that. We find ourselves in the right place at the right time. We can create personal growth and business opportunities.

Craig McCaw, founder of McCaw Cellular, and now Teledesic, conveys his experience:

1. Madeline L'Engle, *A Circle of Quiet* (New York: Harper & Row, 1972) 80.

> You arrive at a moment in time when an entrepreneur, a technology, and the needs of people coincide. You get serendipity every once in a while. You try to be willing to accept it when it works in your behalf.[2]

What McCaw is telling us is that he is aware of time and the incidence of coincidence; that it can be a humbling yet sometimes an uneasy experience; and that it stretches one's comfort level because it is beyond planning and preparation. You may say, "What about luck? Couldn't he just say luck instead of serendipity?" I think he is talking about something much larger than luck; luck connotes an event happening to you, without any competence, desire, market research, or attention paid to advancing technology. I don't think that is what McCaw is telling us here. My interpretation of his quote is that as an entrepreneur you need to pay attention to when things come together at the right place in the right time. You have to be willing to accept it when it comes, to not only be aware of it, but to accept these occasions like a gift. Do something with the gift you have been given. I think of Margaret Wheatley's comment: "Why does progress, when it appears, so often come from unexpected places, or as a result of surprises or serendipitous events that our planning had not considered?"[3]

Another entrepreneur, Brian Tracy, describes synchronicity as:

> Several events conspire together, seemingly totally unrelated, and yet, when they meet together, they form a pattern or bring us the result we were looking for. And we've all had the occasion, where a whole series of things seem to conspire together into a happy coincidence . . . to bring the thing we are looking for.[4]

2. Andrew Kupfer, "Craig McCaw Sees an Internet in the Sky," *Fortune*, May 27, 1996, 62.

3. Margaret Wheatley, *Leadership and the New Science: Learning about Organization from an Orderly Universe* (San Francisco: Berrett-Koehler, 1992) 1.

4. Brian Tracy, *The Psychology of Achievement* (Chicago: Nightingale-Conant, 1984) cassette no. 5.

Not only a "happy coincidence" but a meaningful one. What Tracy is essentially getting at here is the element of coincidence being positive, that it is what we want to happen or a response to a personal wish. We are happy, relieved, and appreciative when things come together and work out. The meaningful thing is that it meets our expectations, our hopes, and takes away some of our worries, at least in the present moment.

Authors of books about synchronicity also have their own definitions. Joseph Jaworski, author of *Synchronicity, The Inner Path of Leadership,* calls these conspiring events "predictable miracles."[5] He sees these experiences "as a product of embracing commitment and surrender, that what we are emotionally impelled to complete will happen as a part of our journey." The surrender has to do with what Jaworski calls "a paradoxical integrity of surrender, surrendering into commitment: I actualize my commitment by listening, out of this my 'doing' arises. Sometimes the greatest acts of commitment involve doing nothing but sitting and waiting until I just know what to do next." Sometimes waiting before responding is the best action. David Peat calls synchronicity the "bridge between matter and mind," in a book of the same name. Peat explains that synchronicity is a bridge that connects the interior and exterior world, or what we just referred to as the inner psychic state and the outer physical manifestation. Jungian analyst Jean Shinoda Bolen named her book *Synchronicity: The Tao of Psychology,* and uses an Agatha Christie metaphor to approach these "clues that point to the existence of an underlying connecting principle."[6] Dr. Bolen asks us, "Is it *commenting* on an inner situation? Is it a metaphor for something going on in my life?"[7] When we accept the idea of synchronicity, every unusual event invites us to pause and reflect on it. Synchronicity does point to something we need to pay

5. Joseph Jaworski, *Synchronicity: The Inner Path of Leadership* (San Francisco: Berrett-Koehler, 1996) 175.

6. Jean Shinoda Bolen, *The Tao of Psychology: Synchronicity and Self* (New York: Harper & Row, 1979) 36.

7. Ibid, p. 30.

attention to, to wake us from some sort of slumber or apathy in our lives. We may doubt the existence of meaningful situations that seem to come from out of the blue and hit us in unexpected ways; we may have a sudden insight, a feeling in our body that is a response to the clash of the deep inner world or state, and the physical world. It shakes perceptions of ourselves. Whichever of the above definitions given by authors speaks to you, all of them reflect that synchronicity can give us direction or inspire us to take a risk, to chart a course, to bring our inner states in concert with what is possible in the outer world.

As you read this book, consider specific instances of synchronicity gleaned from entrepreneurs' interviews reflecting on their experiences. Synchronicity is not a new or trendy experience, as some people may think. It is not a fad or fancy made to explain unknowable things in a simplistic manner. Not only do synchronistic experiences happen now, but they have played a rich role in the development of many businesses. Here's an example that impacts us today, taken from the developing aviation industry of the 1950s. As you read, think about why this is a meaningful coincidence.

When we travel by airplane, we are concerned with what to pack, how to get to the airport, and if we'll be in time for the plane. Once we have settled on our dates and times with the travel agent or airline, the computer manages the information needed to book and hold the reservations.

The development of the SABRE airline reservation system involves an interesting occurrence of synchronicity. Airline reservations before the 1950s took over an hour to book. One day, a serendipitous meeting on an airplane occurred between two men, who happened to be sitting together. They discovered they both shared the same last name: Smith. One Smith was the President of American Airlines, and the other, a senior sales executive from IBM. They started talking about the problem of reserving seats for customers, and how this problem could be solved. "Thirty days after the 'chance' meeting in the sky, IBM made a proposal, and nine years later, the SABRE system became a reality. . . . [It] handles 1 million passenger names in 24 hours, 900 million phone calls a week, and 4,000 reservation messages per second."[8] The two Smiths may have engaged in their conversation because of their last names, and of course, being seated next to each other. Their interaction and interest and openness sparked a new business that provided not only a change in the effectiveness of a corporation and service to its customers, but changed the face of computing.

Returning to Jung's definition, the "meaningful coincidence" can be seen in the inner state of the participants; President Smith saw that in the "external" world, plane reservations were bogging down the advancement of commercial airlines. Reservations were taking an abysmally long time. His "inner state" was desiring an opening, mulling over opportunities to advance the industry. One of those ways was to make things easier for the passengers and efficient for the staff completing travel arrangements. Sales Director Smith was, in his inner state, looking for business opportunities for IBM. He was probably also wondering how he could advance the use of computers into the business world that had been exclusive to military settings. So, both had inner psychic states enabling the experience to happen. In the external world, they were sitting next to each other with the same last names, something which opened themselves up to join in a conversation, that eventually led to that new business venture. The meaning of these events seems perfectly normal in that both wanted to advance themselves, the companies they represented, and the industries they worked within. Yet the outcome may seem to some surreal (how did this happen so smoothly, when I sometimes work on prospective customers for years before they buy!), and that's what makes synchronicity hard to believe, or hard to believe *in*. Synchronicity is elusive, and cannot be controlled as we want to control it.

Another element worth noting here is the gateway between the inner psychic state and the outer physical manifestation. That gateway is openness. Both Smiths had the openness to relate to

---

8. James Burke, *Connections 2* (New York: Ambrose Video, 1994).

each other. Either one of them could have disappeared behind the newspaper or been reviewing a stack of reports, or either one of them could have been thinking about a spectrum of other topics. But they didn't. For whatever reason, they were ready to be engaged in conversation and did so. You may ask here, "So why is this important to me? I sit by people in the plane all the time. Sometimes I am open to talking, and they don't want to talk with me. Or, after a while, I can see the conversation going nowhere and I don't want to talk with them anymore. Isn't this an everyday part of selling? What makes synchronicity different than a routine sales call?"

What makes it different here is that there are many coincidences in life, especially in sales when you are meeting so many people as a part of work. But the synchronicity here is that all four elements are happening at the same time. We can put these four elements into a series of questions to determine if an event is a synchronistic experience:

1. Are the inner and outer states in both people meshing? Yes, we see that both Smiths want to advance their prospective industries, are thinking about it, and acting on their direction.
2. Is it a coincidence? Yes, it has an element of surprise, an unplanned event.
3. Does it come together in time and space? Yes, the Smiths are sitting next to each other on the airplane.
4. Is it meaningful? Yes, meaningfulness is there in that they are both engaged, impassioned about their work. It is surprising to them to be sitting next to each other, and each needs to solve a problem for the other. This joining together is deeply meaningful not only to them, but to the product that came out of their meeting. It is not merely a traditional "hi, how are you" sales call. Nor is it "magic."

Another example that will help illustrate Jung's concept happened to the creators of The Republic of Tea, a San Francisco purveyor of quality teas. Two men shared a ride to the airport, participants in the same conference. One person, a seasoned entrepreneur from California, decided to leave the East-coast conference early, to return to his family. The other, enthusiastic and new to the entrepreneurial world, needed to leave the conference early because he was catching a flight to the South-west. They started talking in the taxi, discovered common interests, and at the airport they arranged to have adjoining seats on the plane. Because their interest in tea was so consuming, they paid little attention to the other events on the plane until they noticed that they had landed in Los Angeles. It was almost as if they were sealed in a cocoon and the rest of the world went away. Soon after, they started the first of many rounds of faxes that eventually led to their company's beginning.

What the story tells us through Jung's ideas is that here are two people starting from very different outer events, but in the taxicab and then on the airplane they discover similar inner states. What is even more striking is that the two entrepreneurs are at different stages in their lives. One of the men, Mel Ziegler, along with his wife Patricia, created the retail clothing store, The Banana Republic. Mel had been reflecting that even though he felt good about Banana Republic, he also felt that "something was left undone." He also felt that business could be part of a positive social change. He said:

> I had always had strong feelings about building a sane and equitable society, but I had found that integrating those feelings with the challenges of an explosive, growing business was an exasperating experience.[9]

The other person, Bill Rosenzweig, a young entrepreneur, was hungry to create a business that would, in Mel's words "find the medium in the real world that would give his essence full expression."[10] These two were so open to each other, so receptive to

9. Mel Ziegler, Patricia Zeigler, and Bill Rosenzweig, *The Republic of Tea* (New York: Currency Doubleday, 1992) 8.
10. Ibid, p. 10.

discussing their ideas, that they were oblivious to the outer events going on inside the plane. The author and entrepreneur Ziegler describes the experience of energy as "The Idea had been born—in us."[11] To take the openness a step further, you must know that Mel was not really interested in starting another business. "I had no interest in going around the track again, life was much too pregnant with possibilities to bother with proving to anybody, especially myself, that given a second chance I could really do it right, but still . . . there was all that hard-earned knowledge, all that roughed-up experience, all that finely honed intuition . . ."[12] This is an important part of understanding synchronicity; it is not always what we think of as magical, nor will everything be exactly the way we want it and fall into place for us. We must have the desire, the openness, the receptivity to work with these situations that bring us forward, to work though the business planning stages. Synchronicity gives us a hand up the ladder once we're willing to accept it—but we have to start and keep climbing to reach our goal. Successful entrepreneurs hold a paradox, one we will scratch the surface of here but will talk about in depth in Part II.

This paradox is working with competency, that is, having the skills needed to be a good entrepreneur, *and* the ability to have wisdom about factors that cannot be measured in traditional ways. One of these factors is the awareness of synchronicity. This awareness, again, is not luck or fate. We must develop both parts of this paradox to be not just good entrepreneurs, but excellent ones. Peter Senge, in *The Fifth Discipline*, has a wonderful description of why intuition and reason are both important to us in decision making. Just as we have two eyes, two ears, two legs, the balance of the two can make us go even further than if we have only one of them: two eyes gives us depth perception; two ears, hearing direction; two legs, quick locomotion. It is essential that we develop both of

11. Ibid, p. 7.
12. Ibid, p. 9.

these areas—intuition and reason—to be entrepreneurs. We'll talk about Senge's description in Part II.

SYNCHRONICITY AS DEFINED BY ENTREPRENEURS

How would other entrepreneurs describe this feeling of "the idea being born"? How do current business owners describe synchronicity?

As part of the doctoral study in leadership I alluded to earlier, I gathered a group of entrepreneurs to survey. I believe that entrepreneurs, as a whole, are business leaders who have a different style of leadership than people who do not own their own business. Being an entrepreneur and being with entrepreneurs, I wanted to study how our lives and decision-making patterns create this style of leadership. I longed to know the incidence and the effects of synchronicity as a part of the creation or start-up phase of business. I knew from my experience that these instances happened to me.

In one business, For The Record, I consulted with private firms and government agencies in building records management programs. When I told people at social gatherings what I did for a living, and I told them I was an entrepreneur, many times the first thing out of their mouths was "How can you stand not knowing who your next client will be?" which usually meant "How do you deal with cash flow problems?" Actually, what started to happen is that I would get phone calls from prospective clients one or two weeks before I ended my current contract. I was astounded that this worked on a regular basis. I began to wonder how this affected other entrepreneurs when they were in the start-up phase of their business. This phase of business is where the "rubber meets the road," where ideas become reality, and every successful business has gone through it whether the company is five or 105 years old.

This is the phase where the founders are tested, employees adjust to high periods of growth, where educating your target market becomes critical, and the incidence for business down-turn is high. As entrepreneurs, it is when we do a lot of wonder-ing if this is really the path we want to walk. Different sources have different definitions of what this phase is, but for my pur-poses, I looked at the creation phase as being the first four years of business. I set out to prove that these coincidences do have relevance and that they affect the decisions made by the entre-preneur, and also affect other stakeholders that are in contact with these leaders: their employees, families, stockholders, ven-dors, communities, and on a global scale. I wanted to know the answers to the these questions:

- Did they base their decision to go into business by looking only at the hard facts on the business or feasibility plan? Or did something happen inside to reflect their desire to be in business?
- Did intuitive thinking (or gut feeling) play a part in making the decision whether or not to go into business?
- Did they meet the "right person at the right time," and did it influence their decision to start their business?
- Did the opportunity to be in business happen at the same time a technology or process became available? How did it affect them? Was the appearance of technology a coinci-dence or a meaningful coincidence?

What I found out during the course of the interviews was not only did synchronicity occur in the start-up phase, but it was valued as a common event in their business lifecycle—spanning from three years to over ten. Some of them told me that synchro-nicity is something that happens to them "almost every day." For example, Margery Miller, president of Miller & Associates in Dallas, Texas, told me that hiring people was one area in which synchronicity worked, that she had hired a salesperson and an office manager by being open and aware of people. She had also gotten clients in unusual ways, from being on an airplane to attending a Christmas party and even networking with a fitness trainer.

In general, commonalities that the entrepreneurs described were that synchronicity assisted them in decision making, and that these events are crossroads, both in the life of a business and where the inner thoughts and feelings of the entrepreneur meet with external events.

Specifically, these entrepreneurs tended to describe synchronicity in the following ways. One way was around the idea of "a series of events that take me to the next step, the life path," and another was that "synchronicity happens when I'm in synch with what I'm supposed to be doing." These two ideas have to do with synchronicity as a way for guidance along their business and life path.

Other entrepreneurs made comments that have to do with synchronicity working in their lives. One described synchronicity as "events that happen in close proximity, manifest in a timely manner." Brazilian entrepreneur Tamas Makray, founder of Promon, an engineering, electronics, and project management company feels that these events have a time restriction, an urgency to act within a certain time frame. Synchronicity is an "extraordinary set of circumstances, lasting only for a short time, like opening a window, giving opportunities for development." He also would describe it as "meeting people, unexpectedly, collaborators, customers, partners, at the time of decisions or options." Another entrepreneur saw synchronicity as a mirror of the inner and exterior worlds: "An internal deliberation with an external event."

This is echoed by Greg Steltenpohl, founder of Odwalla, Inc., a natural beverage manufacturer. He defines synchronicity as "an intersection of external events which line up to point a direction or an intersection of two or more people whose thoughts coincide simultaneously." We can see this in the story of the two Smiths on the flight whose meeting sparked the creation of SABRE computer system.

Entrepreneur Paul Hawken, founder of Smith & Hawken, the garden supply retailer, also gives as an example of matching an idea with its intended group of customers. Again, this is a situation of matching the paradox of competence, balancing your business skills with the ability to be aware of both your inner state and the external environment.

> Luck or no, Smith & Hawken has had so many good breaks that we sometimes ascribe our fate to a great measure of good fortune. My wife asked me early on how the business was doing, and I replied that it seemed as if a guardian angel were hovering above us. Our timing was inadvertently perfect: the baby boomers were settling down, buying houses, and becoming interested in gardening . . .[13]

Paul's quote may throw some of you off with his talk of luck and angels, but keep open to what he has to say. Look at this as more than merely a lucky coincidence. Apply the questions of synchronistic experiences that we have covered: Is it a coincidence? Is it meaningful? Is Hawken's inner state reflecting with those of his customers? How about the outer outcomes of the inner experiences?

We can also view Hawken's comments through McCaw's statement: What came together for him through an entrepreneur, technology, and the needs of people coinciding. Hawken is the entrepreneur with the knowledge, the ability to run a business; the technology of mail order and distribution have developed to include express delivery services; and needs of the people are met by having a catalog so they don't have to go out during a regular work day, but can order conveniently, choosing their purchases at home.

SHADES OF SYNCHRONICITY

I want to revisit Jung's definition of synchronicity. He said that synchronicity is a *meaningful coincidence between an inner psychic state and an outward physical manifestation or event*. In addition to Jung's and the entrepreneurs' definitions, it is helpful to explore

13. Paul Hawken, *Growing a Business* (New York: Simon & Schuster, 1987) 148.

synchronicity from the semantic point of view, the dictionary description of synchronicity's cousins: chance, coincidence, serendipity, and grace. Each has a nuance, or shade that makes it different from the rest.

Chance is defined in *Webster's* as "risk, apparent absence of cause or design, destiny . . . the ratio of a thing happening to its not happening."[14] Chance takes into account the mathematical probability of an event. You have a one in fifty-two chance of drawing a certain card from a card deck or a different set of odds in winning the state lottery. Chance is different than synchronicity because it focuses mainly on mathematical probability rather than the inner state or the external event, and it does not emphasize meaningful experiences.

Coincidence is "an accidental or remarkable occurrence of events."[15] This term is more concerned with events that happen at the same time that point to a causal relationship. Causal relationships are based on action and reaction; if action A happens, then it causes outcome B to happen. Jung discovered that synchronicity is acausal, that it works differently than a causal relationship. Outcome C could happen, which would be surprisingly different from outcome B. Chance is close to synchronicity, but it still lacks the "meaningful coincidence" aspect of synchronicity.

Serendipity is an "aptitude for making fortunate discoveries accidentally"[16] and is discovered more than manifested. You go to a friend's house and discover on her table some travel plans she is making that would be helpful to you for a business trip you are taking next month, which you haven't thought through yet. Or you happen to see an old friend in a distant city where you are traveling, and she knows a friend you could contact for an opportunity. Serendipity seems to have meaningfulness, yet lacks the inner psychic state that synchronicity demands.

14. N. Webster, *Webster's New Twentieth Century Dictionary of the English Language, Second Edition* (San Francisco: Collins World, 1975) 301.

15. Ibid, p. 353.

16. Ibid, p. 1656.

For some, synchronicity has a spiritual dimension. "Miracle," "divine intervention," and "grace" are ways of naming the experience. *Miracle*, bathing at Lourdes, France, and being healed from an infirmity is an example that defies all logic and probability and produces something surprising, or against all common acceptance. *Divine intervention* is the working of a higher power or divine source that intervenes in our affairs to assist us, many times in ways we do not expect. At times, we can feel other people are acting as benevolent beings looking out for our best interests. Some of us may have an "otherworldly feeling" that something bigger than us is present but not in the physical form we are used to seeing. *Grace* can be defined as an unearned blessing, something that benefits us, that is given freely. We may count chance encounters as grace, but the key word here is that grace is unearned. Grace can show itself at work when an employee needs to be reprimanded for a repeated mistake. For example, the employee continues to talk to friends on the phone instead of finishing a report that you need to have for a marketing meeting at three. This isn't the first time the employee has done this. Grace is the space between calling the employee into your office, and taking in the breath you start the conversation with. Instead of being very upset and showing it in an inappropriate way, you have been graced with patience to hear his or her point of view and thus deal with the issue diplomatically and effectively.

All three terms, miracle, divine intervention, and grace, have a religious or spiritual context. Many instances could be considered synchronistic, but it all depends on the perception of the person involved in the event. Some people will say that it is the "Hand of God" that has a work in our lives. We'll discover in Chapter 3 that many entrepreneurs will blur the boundaries of what is synchronicity and what is grace. An example of a graced moment that protected me from a life-threatening situation went like this.

I was driving down the freeway to Seattle through high-speed traffic on a Saturday afternoon. Suddenly, three cars ahead of me, the driver slammed on the brakes. All the cars behind the first one stopped suddenly, and the car behind me quickly responded by swerving onto the shoulder, passing my car. No car hit another. The feeling was one of a buffer between the car ahead and the car behind me that protected my vehicle from damage and myself from being severely hurt. It was a miracle that there was no crash, no injuries, especially since the cars were all going 60 miles per hour.

To me, that was a graced moment, as I was protected from a group of cars going from a high rate of speed to a dead stop in a matter of seconds. The person behind me had the skill to move around my vehicle and stop before he hit the concrete median. No one behind us ran into us, either. There was a feeling of being protected in a shell—something larger than myself—and I knew I wasn't going to get hurt. At this point I will allude to a Jungian term: *numinous*. There are times that people have the feeling of a shell, a bubble of light, a cocoon of radiance surrounding them at, usually, very important events. I felt a shell of protection in this situation, felt that I did not get hurt because I was surrounded in this bubble. These events can be a part of synchronicity, or if we give the credit to God or a higher power, a graced experience.

SYNCHRONICITY REDEFINED AND REFINED

To reach our own working definition of synchronicity we can incorporate all we've discussed—the definitions from Jung, from entrepreneurs, and our study of semantics—and can extrapolate some commonalties from all of them:

> The **relationship and interplay between internal thoughts and feelings with outer events** is important. The inner thought is meaningful to the outer event and the outer event is meaningful to the inner thought.
> The intersection of **time and space** plays a factor.
> A synchronistic event surpasses the **probability of chance**.
> The event has to be **meaningful**.

Pulling these elements into a sentence or statement can create the following definition: *Synchronicity is an event or series of events when the external and internal worlds affect each other, making meaningful experiences that change our lives.*

Applying the above, let's hear two historical stories from Carl Jung, and compare the events with our redefinition of synchronicity.

JUNG'S GOLDEN SCARAB

As Jung said, synchronicity is "a meaningful coincidence of two or more events where something other than the probability of chance is involved."[17] The incident itself has to be meaningful to the person who is experiencing these events. In his writings on synchronicity, Jung describes two stories that illustrate this meaningfulness: the golden scarab story and the plum pudding events.

The golden scarab story unfolds in Jung's office, where he is working with a young woman. Emotionally guarded and protective of herself, Jung is having a particularly difficult time with her, trying to break through her resistance to treatment. She begins to describe a dream. In it, she is given a golden scarab. As she recalls more details about the dream, Jung hears a tapping on the office window from the outside. He opens the window, and catches the insect as it flies across the room. It is a beetle that is the closest relative to the scarab in the geographic area. He shows the beetle to the woman, and because the inner thought (describing the dream of the beetle) and the actual appearance of the beetle occurred, her reaction is one of shock, and her resistance changes. She had been emotionally "jolted," as it were, and she was then able to continue therapy successfully. Here, the elements of synchronicity play themselves out with our new definition:

Synchronicity is an event or series of events when the external and internal worlds affect each other, making meaningful experiences that change our lives.

17. Carl Jung, *Synchronicity: A Causal Connecting Principal* (Princeton, NJ: Princeton University Press, 1960) 104.

The appearance of the beetle (external) and the discussion of the dream (internal) at the same point in time, created an event; there was the need for a different type of intervention on the part of Jung to influence his patient's healing (changing lives) and this synchronistic event surpassed the probability of chance.

There was also the element of openness. Jung could have ignored the insect at the window; he could have had his ego invested in traditional methods of analysis, trying to get through to his patient, to wedge his foot into the door of her defenses. The patient also could have been closed; she could have continued to ignore the beetle, to say "so what," to continue to befuddle Jung, not wanting to lay her defenses down and trust the situation. But they did not act in these ways and it changed both of their lives.

The above story took place in Jung's office in a relatively short period of time. Other synchronistic experiences can happen over a number of years, as illustrated in the next story.

The plum pudding events revolve around a relationship: a M. Deschamps and a M. deFortigibu, and three unusual events. The first event occurs when deFortigibu gives a young boy, Deschamps, a piece of plum pudding. The second event happens ten years later, when Deschamps orders a piece of plum pudding in a Paris restaurant. However, deFortigibu, who happens to be in the same restaurant, has just ordered the last piece! Many years later the third event in the sequence of events occurs; Deschamps is eating a piece of plum pudding at a party, joking that the only thing lacking is deFortigibu. At that moment, guess who walks in? DeFortigibu had the incorrect address, and had walked in by mistake.

The plum pudding story contains three events, in different spaces (i.e., locations) and time (occurring over a number of years), but all related because of the same two people acting as mirrors at each event; each one of them plays a role around the plum pudding.

Synchronicity can be a guide to decision making. It can help us create a company, build relationships, grow to be creative people, and contribute to our leadership roles in our business and personal lives. Synchronicity can occur as events that shock us out of our slumber and complacency of everyday life, they can be comforting or uncomfortably disquieting, depending on the situations.

Synchronicity can make us:

Aware of a direction to go, as in McCaw's reflection on technology, or Jung's scarab story,

Give us a solution we've been looking for, as in Brian Tracy's words, the story of the two Smiths on the airplane, and

Give deeper meaning to our lives: in a serious way, as in protection from a potentially harmful auto collision; or in a humorous way, as in the case of the plum pudding.

In this chapter, we've built a foundation. We've reached a workable definition of synchronicity as an event or series of events when the external and internal worlds affect each other, making meaningful experiences that change our lives. For the skeptics, I hope I've convinced you to prop open the door of interest a little more. I encourage you to stay open, stay interested, because the following chapter will further demonstrate the influence of synchronicity in general life situations and how it has manifested itself in the entrepreneurial world. We'll go on to discovering stories about synchronicity, through life situations, then through the eyes of entrepreneurs.

QUESTIONS

1. What situations have you experienced where synchronicity might have taken place?
2. How can you look at them through the four elements of synchronicity: meaningfulness, coincidence, inner psychic state, and outer physical manifestation?

3. Do you have friends who value synchronicity? What about those who are skeptical?
4. How do you make decisions in your life?

As Peter Senge mentioned earlier, we use balance when we consider synchronistic experiences. We consider the event, the source or person, and our own intentions. Sometime on a business trip you may go where Zeigler and Rosenzwieg went: straight into starting a business. Or it may be something in a conversation you had; for example, a person mentioned a particular author to me I hadn't heard of, and the same author was also mentioned in another book I cracked open the next day, a book that was unrelated to the author's discipline or work. What may be even more of an improbability was that this book was a devotional, with a page to read and reflect upon every day. And on that day, August 6th, the name of the author I had just heard about was included in the devotional reading for that day.

Chapter 2
Synchronicity Changes Lives

Psychologist and conflict resolution consultant Arnold Mindell of the Process Work Center in Portland, Oregon observed in his dissertation that "Synchronicity occurs as prefaces to the creation or annihilation of existence."[1] I would translate that to mean that synchronicity occurs in situations that have to do with extreme life changes: meeting your mate, someone dying, or in a crisis situation. In these times in our lives, we feel our vulnerability. We feel out of control, in good ways, uncomfortable ways, or perhaps a little of both. We seek answers from places where we may not have looked before. We are open to possibilities because we feel great joy, feel a state of flow that goes on and on, or closed to opportunity when we experience great pain, open like a raw wound, and grief that won't go soon enough. It appears when we seem to take a large risk in our inner lives to experience the risks of being open, being vulnerable; things unexpected will be there for us. The investment we make in pushing our inner sense of self could become the answer to a dilemma we've been thinking about for some time.

1. Arnold Mindell, *An Investigation of the Unitary Background Patterning Synchronistic Phenomena* (Cincinnati, OH: Union Graduate School, 1976) 20.

This answer or a "piece of the puzzle" might give us information we are seeking, could come from a stranger, a sign on the road, or a sentence in a book.

We're going to take a look at stories of people's lives, to see how synchronistic events that play in our lives—again those instances being points in time where things "fit together" in a series of events—are an intimate side of a vast universe of possibilities and probabilities. Synchronicity makes our attitudes about what is possible expand and a whole new life comes forward, and many times changes our direction. I am reminded of Jung's observation about the meeting of people sometimes being like a chemical reaction; when they come together, both are transformed.

The stories you are about to read focus on different times of life that are common to us all, times with which we can easily identify. The "meeting your mate" story is about synchronicity playing a primary part in a love story. The "finding my ancestors" story is where the search for roots, and family history, uncovers the bones of synchronicity. The last section of stories has to do with crisis situations in our lives. Crisis situations are just that, where we feel on the edge and can't see any answers to our dilemma. Sometimes the anxiety has to do with a personal crisis where one can feel so vulnerable and up against the sharpest edge that only two choices seem to be options: a breakdown or a breakthrough. Another type of crisis is when we are up against a financial wall; many entrepreneurs told me that there were times they thought they would lose their business and then money came from various sources, sometimes on the exact day it was needed. The sources in these cases were family members, friends, and acquaintances. But synchronicity's "hand" was there to support not only the business with cash flow, but reassure the entrepreneur with a continual source of an inner sense of support.

At this point some of you may be thinking skeptically, "What is this synchronicity thing? I don't believe in it! What kind of rumors are you spreading?"

One of the entrepreneurs I interviewed commented that he didn't think there was such a thing as synchronicity, because if there were, there would have to be antisynchronistic experiences. But does there have to be? Do our thoughts have to have an either/or existence? If we have something, do we have to expect its opposite to be present as well? If we see things in either red or blue, do we miss the value in what purple can give us? Can we understand that synchronistic experiences happen, the good or bad connotations we are given can change in time, and later the real purpose will unfold? I have some ways of explaining it, while at other times wonder if it can be "pinned down" at all. Sometimes words can't describe the feelings, emotions, and outcomes of these events, but words are what I have to explain what I know and have experienced through myself or other people. People ask me "Why did this or that happen to me? Isn't the outcome of synchronicity always supposed to be good? If a bad thing happens, why didn't synchronicity warn me so I wouldn't get hurt?" At these times, I think of what Deja Shoe founder Julie Lewis, creator of the shoe made from recycled materials told me; "Synchronistic experiences can sometimes lead you off the 'right' path—but it is usually to teach you something you needed to learn before you can get back on the right path; but I still believe synchronistic 'hunches' should be followed, regardless."

What about the appropriateness of looking for synchronistic events? We know people can go to the other extreme, and can go overboard with their dependence on synchronicity so that it seems that they stop functioning. It's as if these extremists have displaced their own personal responsibility and control of events in their lives. Everything that happens begins to have an overabundant meaning to them, they try to read a lot through and between the lines, making you feel paranoid about what you say around them. This is true for any phenomenon—what we don't understand fully can be twisted, or we can become so dependent on something that we try to control it, or surrender our power to it. It's like relationships that are powerful to us. An example would be in a mentorship situation. The ideal situation is to have the mentor see the potential in the mentoree, and to assist them with their development. The unhealthy position is to have the mentoree become too dependent on the mentor's judgment and accept what the mentor says without thinking for themselves.

Still, the gift of synchronicity is that it does change our lives, and in so doing doesn't negate our personal control over a situation. The following stories illustrate the events that change our perceptions, that wake us up, and that show us that there is something much bigger than we are that has a play in this universe.

MEETING YOUR MATE

One day, Gabrielle received a letter from Gram, a high school sweetheart. Even though they had kept in touch occasionally over the years since graduation, they pursued different lives. Gabrielle lives in New York City, and Gram's letter arrived postmarked from Washington, D.C. After reading the news about his life, she wondered to herself how it would be to have him visit, to see him again, and talk over old times.

For some reason, Gabrielle was compelled to show this letter to her landlady, someone she didn't have that much in common with and didn't see much at all. The landlady read the letter and, surprisingly, responded, "We need to take a walk." Moments later she and Gabrielle were walking down Broadway in Manhattan. At a doorway, she stopped Gabrielle and motioned, "We need to go into this art gallery." Gabrielle was puzzled when the landlady didn't give an explanation, but went in anyway. When Gabrielle turned the corner, there was Gram, the person she received the letter from a scant two hours ago, staring back at her in surprise.

Gabrielle was understandably shocked. She had no idea Gram was in Manhattan and he had not contacted her about visiting her during his stay in New York, nor mentioned it in the letter. As far as she had known, he was comfortably in his home in Washington, D.C.!

What makes this story so amazing is the many events that seem past the possibility of chance. The envelope of time that elapsed, from opening the letter to seeing the person right in front of her, was less than two hours. The urge to share with the landlady a letter on a certain day was uncommon, as was letting the landlady convince her to take a walk.

Gabrielle could have turned down her landlady's insistence that they go for a stroll. "Are you crazy, I'm not going for a walk today," could have been something she said. She could have thrown the letter across the room or filed it in a drawer to look at later. But I bet she was probably thinking of Gram, reminiscing. Isn't it curious that the landlady happened to be home that day, a day she wasn't usually home? It would have taken only one event, one link, to throw the rest of the chain off.

This may be a good time to discuss an element essential to synchronicity, and that is *openness*, that our inner psychic minds are open to what is possible. We may have days where we are looking for new adventures and we are wide open, like at a networking breakfast, or when friends we've known for years come over to dinner. We may be more or less guarded at a performance review or a critical meeting where we will be judged by our performance. Our awareness has different settings like a thermostat, depending on our alertness, life situation, depression, enthusiasm, trust in ourselves and others, and even how much sleep we've had the night before. Gabrielle was open to possibilities by agreeing to take a walk. Whatever was scheduled that day took a back seat to the adventure of walking where the landlady was to go. The landlady's insistence and secretiveness must have played a role in seducing Gabrielle into stepping out of what she had to do that day.

I am reminded of Tai Babilonia's description of pairs figure skating as recounted by Carol Frenier: "With some embarrassment [Tai] explained to the television interviewer that her coach had told her that her partner's job was to present her, and that her job was to allow herself to be presented."[2] And we have to wonder, is this part of synchronicity's job? To present us? And is our job to be open as much as possible, to be able to be presented?

Joe Jaworski has a touching story about meeting his wife Mavis for the first time at an airport. They happened to pass each other on the way to separate flights, and something inside him told him to stop her, to tell her that he didn't know why, but he just needed to speak with her. He did follow her, stop her, and tell her that he didn't know why, he just had to speak with her. She stopped, gave Joe her business card, and boarded her plane.

He could have shut down that inner voice, he could have come up with a plethora of excuses not to talk to her; to approach this woman he had never seen before to engage her in conversation was too inappropriate, too weird, "what if she tells me I'm crazy, she calls security, or she ignores me, and I will feel ashamed, crazy, threatened and rejected." He could have continued, "This is so unlike me to walk up to some total stranger and strike up a conversation. Here I am with my son and we have to catch a plane to visit a college, something very important to both of us. To botch this special time together would be hurtful." Mavis, on the other hand, also could have also come up with many responses to derail this event. She could have demanded, "Who are you? Leave me alone, you're crazy, who do you think you are?" Amazingly, however, both of them were open to the moment, open to the situation and assessing the cues from each other. They only had a moment. What is fascinating as well is that she knew she would meet a man of importance on this trip. That was the condition of her inner psychic state.

It might make us consider how we think about our wishes and dreams and how some of them come true. Has it ever happened that you are thinking about someone and the phone rings and there they are on the other end of the line? What are the implications of us wanting something and having elements of

2. Carol Freiner, *Business and the Feminine Principle: The Untapped Resource* (Boston: Butterworth-Heinemann, 1997) 168.

people, places, and time start working together to meet those needs? Can our desires, coupled with our commitment to something, expedite these experiences?

For instance, I'd always wanted to know my family history, to research my ancestors, where they lived, what challenges they had to overcome, and what they looked like. For several years I had read about my great-great grandparents and family crossing the Oregon Trail in the mid-1800s. I wondered where they had settled when they reached Oregon, and what did the landscape look like?

FINDING MY ANCESTORS

Driving through the Willamette Valley to Eugene, Oregon, I was heading for a job interview. I had started my journey at four in the morning from Seattle, and it was about nine when I reached Salem, an hour north of Eugene. I was noticing the landscape, the rolling hills that followed the black ribbon of freeway. How similar they looked to the undulating Palouse Hills where I grew up. It then occurred to me that my ancestors who crossed the Oregon Trail settled in the Willamette Valley. While I mused about it for a little while, the thought soon vanished, replaced with a dialogue in my head, questions and answers anticipated in the job interview.

After the interview on the drive back to Seattle, the thought of the rolling hills came back to me. I found myself saying out loud, "The first freeway exit that advertises a museum, I'll pull over." I was surprised at the strength of my resolve. Within two miles was a sign for the Brownsville museum, and as I turned to go into town, I was thinking how crazy an idea this was, and that I could still turn around at any moment. I stopped at the museum and asked if there were some sort of archives there. The attendant said, "No, but the genealogist is here," and she pointed to the back of the museum. My feet dragged like lead up the stairs, not yet convinced that this detour would bear any fruit. I asked about my great-great grandfather and his children who settled in the Valley, his wife having died on the Oregon Trail.

He opened several index card boxes, until he came to my great-great-grandfather's name, and suddenly became very excited. "Do you know much about your ancestor?" he asked, "because we just have his name, but not where he died or much about him." I told him what I knew. He then said, "Go to the drug store around the corner and get a map." I did, and when I returned he drew in the property lines of the homestead. I drove out to the property where my ancestor settled, something I'd always wanted to know, with the realization that the day had started with a completely different focus: a journey to an interview.

How did I know that something I had wanted for a long time was going to happen? I didn't, but even so it did happen since I was present to the moment. I followed up on the hunch that concurred with a bodily response that felt involuntary. What was the determining factor able to sway my decision to get off of the freeway? What about the voice saying "Are you crazy?"

Another part of synchronicity is being in the *present moment*. This is difficult when you work within the context of the future, as in strategic planning, or in the past, as in archives work that is based in history. Being in the moment is essential for picking up subtle cues and clues.

A woman I know had just lost her mother a scant year ago, and her father a few years earlier. Still grieving, she found herself wondering out loud about her roots now that she was the elder of her family. She mentioned it to a group of people in a room at work one morning. I was on the phone, but I thought I heard her mention something about her grandparents being from the Matanuska Valley in Alaska. I thought I might have been wrong, listening to many conversations at once, but I took the chance and asked her, "Did you say Matanuska Valley?" "Yes," she replied. My curiosity was aroused since I don't know a lot of people who know about this Valley, a colony created during the "New Deal" of the Franklin Roosevelt administration, unless they are from Alaska, are historians, or lived at the time of the New Deal.

What turned out to be a casually overheard remark was taking a dramatic turn, and would be a life-changing experience for her. After talking a few minutes and making a few phone calls, she and I both found out that her grandparents and my partner's parents were neighbors! She decided *that day* that she would be traveling to Alaska to find her roots, something she had previously thought about, but not with much seriousness. As I write this, she is on her way to Alaska to take on her role as the elder of her family.

There are times of crisis, when decisions that affect us have to happen in a short amount of time. These can happen in our business and personal relationships, in business situations, and in our relationship to our environment. Several people have told me that synchronicity happens more to them, or that they are more aware of it, in crisis situations. I asked one restaurateur if he thought it happened more during crisis situations. Ron Paul's reply, "To be in the restaurant business *is* to be in crisis!"

"I guarantee it" is the mantra of The Men's Wearhouse. Exuberant entrepreneur George Zimmer, retailer of men's fine suits, tells us a story of a critical time in his business. "During the oil crisis in Houston in the early 1980s we did not have sufficient operating capital to run the business, which could have led to our going out of business. A series of fortuitous events that could be described as synchronistic between myself, my mother, and my grandfather provided the needed capital." He reflects, "Primarily, synchronicity has occurred when the right person has appeared at the right time!"

Another crisis story has to do with a personal crisis—being called as a leader. At times we are called to be more than we think we can be, to stretch our frame of reference about ourselves. We are invited in different ways to take parts in leading families or organizations, taking responsibility for our world, and following our unique callings. Sometimes these invitations are not easy to take: it means shouldering responsibilities we may not want, but feel we need to carry, and do well; it means acting for the sake of others, and sometimes being criticized for it. I call these times when we decide whether or not to accept an invitation a time of *personal crisis*.

DREAMING OF K'ROUGE

I was in the first year of my doctorate program in leadership. The three-year cycle of studies focused on personal leadership the first year, organizational leadership the second, and global leadership in the third. As the coursework of the first year went on, we saw and discussed closely the lives of many leaders.

I had the realization that many leaders died either by assassination or had died many deaths of self by imprisonment "of their own thoughts," meaning enslaving of their own perceptions of themselves, deaths of relationships with others by betrayal, and the deaths of dreams, ideas, and actions.

As a part of the introductory class, I was reading the journeys of leaders as varied as Gandhi and Amelia Earhart. I began to question my role as a leader and whether I would be willing to lose my life or parts of myself for what I believed in. Was I committed enough to think of myself as a leader? Did I have the skills to do seemingly insurmountable tasks? What was I doing? The more I reflected, the more I realized these incessant questions were highlighting all of the vulnerable places in myself, nagging me to work on those places, even though I might never achieve the full knowledge of or uncover the meaning to my own life. Was I passionate enough about my work to withstand the hard knocks?

While on a cruise ship a few months later, I had a dream. It was a dream that repeated hand-drawn words in a murky sky: K'red K'red K'red. Then K'rouge. The sky that I saw in the dream was a red watercolor of changing tones and tints that repeated the message, like a movie playing in slow motion. I awoke and wrote it down, puzzling during the few minutes of reflection on what this could mean. Since I was teaching on this ship as part of a conference, I shared the dream with the other teachers at the breakfast table. "What could K'rouge mean?" After a few suggestions, a person at the table said, "Is it something to do with Khmer Rouge?" I didn't know what he was talking about. "You know," he said, "in Cambodia where the leaders were murdered."

As I walked away from the breakfast table and up the stairs, I thought about whom I could talk to about Khmer Rouge. I went up to the top deck of the ship, sat on a hard wooden bench, and wrote notes in my journal for about twenty minutes. Writing in my journal is a way for me to understand what is going on in my life, to go deeper and recall what I have done, replay important times during parts of my life. Tired, I closed the journal and stared at the patterns of the waves reflecting the sunlight. I looked down at the cover of the journal, then opened it to reread the first pages. There before me were the anxiety-filled questions about leadership that I had written a few short months before.

This story ends with a plane flight home from Miami where the cruise ship docked. Next to me on the plane was a former captain who knew about Khmer Rouge, and spoke with me about it. I explained to him about the dream, and not only did he talk to me about Cambodia, but also of his journey as a leader, the times he felt depressed and destitute and what he did about it. He said that he was willing to give up his life for what he believed in, and described how much he cared for the people he was responsible for, even to the point of waiting for them to finish eating before he had his dinner. From our discussion, I found I did have the answers to more of the questions than I thought. This experience gave me more than merely a glimpse of coincidence, it gave me a person's viewpoint on how he worked through some of his doubts to become a strong and caring leader.

Again, there is a series of events that it is important to acknowledge to understand synchronicity. The first event I experienced was the personal crisis of whether or not I should be a leader, continue my doctorate studies, and whether or not this leadership path was something I wanted to follow, for reasons of self-preservation. Next, I had a dream that gave me elusive hints about something that I was open enough to think about as a source of information. I was in the present moment when I talked about the dream at the breakfast table. The pattern repeated when I was on the plane. Still having the crisis about leadership and unsure about the meaning of the dream, I was in the present moment with the former captain, explaining the dream and alluding to my personal crisis. I was changed as a result of those events, which fits our definition of synchronicity as a series of events when the external and internal worlds affect each other, making meaningful experiences that change our lives.

There is yet another element to synchronicity: the *vulnerability* to let these experiences happen to you. Remember the words of Craig McCaw in the first chapter? "You have to be willing to accept it when it comes along." Vulnerability has to happen before acceptance to experience a synchronistic relationship fully. It does not happen only in crisis; when accepting a compliment we must be humble, open, and willing to receive this gift.

The next story—again, one of crisis—has to do with the breakup of a relationship. In it, you can see strength in the vulnerability, and the surprise ending.

VISITOR IN THE GRAND TETONS

For three summers between my four years of undergraduate school I worked in the Grand Teton mountains of northwest Wyoming. I had just broken up with my boyfriend. After our breaking-up talk, I didn't see the future in much of anything, and decided to go for a walk. I went past Jackson Lake Lodge into a familiar grove of trees. Although I was half hidden in this grove, I could still see the lake below and the bluff where there was a viewpoint over the lake. I cried for a while, looking up occasionally for something of comfort to me, some sort of stability in the midst of this confusion: the deep green basin and the ice blue mountains; a regal moose, her calves following; and a young family at the viewpoint, the sprightly young son arrayed in brightly colored clothing, playing on the benches.

I tried to console myself with a litany of thoughts, the trite sentences one repeats in her head after a relationship break-up, over and over, like a continuous tape: "I've got my whole life ahead of me. There are other fish in the sea. There is a future ahead." But I still felt hurt and cold as I watched the sun fall quickly behind those stunning mountains.

I was jolted out of my thoughts by the boy in bright colors standing not far away from me: "You're not supposed to be here by yourself." I looked at him, then over his shoulder to his parents, still at the viewpoint, then back at this boy visitor.

"What?" I said.

"Come back," he repeated. "You are not supposed to be here by yourself."

"Are you serious?" I replied. He looked as impatient as a young boy waiting for ice cream. He didn't leave the place he was standing until I promised that I would come back. Then he turned around and skipped back to his family while my jaw hung open in awe.

How did this young boy know I needed comforting? I did not pass him on the way up the hill. I didn't think anyone could see me clearly, hidden in the trees, so how did he know I was upset? Again, I think openness had a lot to do with this. I did not know what the young man was thinking. But by the way he talked, he was very open and innocent. I can't imagine him talking to people in that way in usual conversation. I can't imagine what he was thinking. But I was certainly glad he came to visit on that August day.

Many might find this story unremarkable or unbelievable, as there are too many holes in the story. "What if the young boy saw you and you were too upset to see him? What if, instead of him running to you, he was just playing and happened upon you? Are you really sure that's what he said, and not what you wanted to hear?" This "devil's advocate" voice is helpful, as it helps us to be honest with our interpretations. Like some people who fish, we are tempted to embellish our tales, to make the fish longer than it really was for the sake of letting others know how much better we are. And yet that is another element to synchronicity that is important: that we all are *honest* with our stories.

When people ask me why synchronicity doesn't occur more often, I usually answer that we haven't developed the four essential elements: openness, being in the present moment, vulnerability, and honesty. Honesty is especially important. Dishonesty closes us down. We cannot participate openly with others if we don't want to stay in the present moment because it hurts too much. Do you know the feeling of having someone know you are lying to their face? How does that feel? People get hurt by others' lack of honesty, but if we are dishonest with ourselves the cost is even higher. We shut off from our own creativity and innocence, and it becomes difficult to relate to events like synchronicity. Vulnerability becomes impossible.

Synchronicity is a partner in the dance of our lives as we sometimes need it. In this chapter, we found instances of synchronicity at play in transition points in our lives. These periods are usually times when we have taken a great risk, have been extremely disappointed, or are in a crisis from which we don't know the way out, but we need the answers now.

Before we end this chapter I'd like to leave you with one last story. Its ending is a mystery to me; however, I speculate on an idyllic ending from time to time.

I was walking with a group of people to retrieve my car for the last leg of my commute. I had offered a ride to three people who needed a lift to their bed and breakfast, something I don't normally do. They told me how kind I was to help them, that this was not a familiar place, and they had felt squeamish asking someone for help.

As we approached the car my heart started racing. I knew something was wrong with the car though I didn't know what, but as I got closer, I noticed that the door was open and one of the back windows had been forced open. I was horrified, but didn't want to alarm my guests. I quietly mentioned to one of the guests what had happened, and getting into the car, I noticed that my tape player was gone. Surprised that I could keep a cheerful conversation going through the shock of having my vehicle burgled, the people in the car kept repeating how grateful they were that I was there, able to help them when they needed it.

It wasn't until later that I realized that the only tape that was stolen was a tape by Dr. Deepok Chopra explaining the concept of karma. I wondered what the probability of having a tape of Deepok talking about the law of karma, being taken from my vehicle, would be. I often wondered if the thieves listened to the tape, and if it changed their lives—if they hadn't known before that "what goes around comes around" and would be enlightened. I may never know. What I do know is that the tape was delivered to whom it needed to be delivered, and it was the exclamation point at the end of the sentence of the day.

REFLECTION QUESTIONS

1. How did you meet a significant person in your life?
2. Recall a crisis situation. Was there someone who appeared and helped you in your time of need? Someone that made it possible for you to achieve what you wanted or what you needed?
3. When traveling, has a stranger come up to you and helped you to find your direction or given you advice?
4. In a significant life transition, such as a birth, a death, a job change, or a divorce, were you stunned by any action by someone you did or didn't know?

How to Develop the Elements of Synchronicity: Openness, Being in the Present Moment, Vulnerability, and Honesty
To Develop Openness: Introduce yourself to a stranger, take an afternoon off and go to a place you don't normally go, eat at a new restaurant or bring home a vegetable you have never had before.

To Develop Being in the Present Moment: Look around you and pay attention to the colors in the room. Pick one and see how many times it occurs in your view.

To Develop Vulnerability: Apologize to a person if you have harmed them. Tell people how much you appreciate them. Tell someone a meaningful story.

To Develop Honesty: Keep mental track of how you "stretch the truth" during the day. How often do you tell the truth? Does it hurt other people when you are not honest with them? How does it affect them when you are honest with them?

Chapter 3
Viewing Synchronicity Through Entrepreneurs' Eyes

In the movie *Field of Dreams*, the characters of Ray and Annie Kinsella weave their way through a series of synchronistic events. In quiet moments while walking through the corn on their farm, Ray hears external voices: "Build it and he will come," "Ease his pain," and "Go the distance." Ray's response to these cryptic callings spurs him to go on a journey and ultimately resolve a deep conflict seeded in his heart: the memories of his deceased father, John, and their influence on Ray's role as a father.

Ray recalls his dad's passion: baseball. While other kids were told of heroes from storybooks, Ray knew baseball heroes as if they were neighbors. His Dad forced him to play until Ray said no, and went off to set his own life and to go as far away from his dad as he could, both geographically and in his values: college at Berkeley, California.

The events that spur Ray to go on a journey come from deep inside of him. One series of events, made up of two scenes, is particularly striking. The first scene has Ray sitting in a gymnasium during a PTA meeting, discussing the censorship of books. In a cacophony of parental, concerned voices, Ray is trying to figure out the latest voice given to him from the corn: "Ease his pain." Ease whose pain, Ray wonders. Ray is doodling on a newspaper, writing the words "ease his pain." While Annie defends Terrance Mann, the author of a book that the crowd wants to ban, Ray continues pondering until he gets it: "Ease his pain" refers to Terrance Mann! So in this first scene, we see his discovery of the first step of the journey, one that puzzles and confuses him. Ray doesn't know the next step, but he does hold one of the clues that will lead to the journey yet to be uncovered.

The second scene in the series of events has Ray and Annie in their home, and he is telling her that he has figured out this Terrance Mann thing. He says at first that he thinks he is supposed to take Terrance Mann to a baseball game, and soon after, he changes his resolve to say he is certain he is supposed to do this. Annie disapproves of this wacky idea, reminds her husband that they have too much going at the farm for him to be running off to follow some crazy idea. Then she stops and asks, "Is Fenway the one with the green wall?" He says yes. She then tells him that she had a dream of Ray taking Terrance to a baseball game at Fenway. Her husband says he had the very same dream. They both scurry to pack the van—and he is gone.

"It's just a movie," you may comment. "Why should I pay attention? Aren't these events just a coincidence?" However, consider that it is more than a coincidence—Ray is keeping his father's memory churning in his mind during all of this. He is in the middle of Iowa, raising his daughter, and questioning his role as a father, in view of his own relationship with his father. He wants to see if he can make peace with the memories of his father, that all his father cared about was baseball and pushing Ray to be a superior athlete. Ray doesn't want to make the same mistakes his father made. Ray has a deep fear of becoming his father, and that is the reason for his journey. This resolution of his inner psychic state will play out with the outer physical manifestation.

The rest of the movie involves even more scenes that are synchronistic, but I will leave it up to you, if you have seen it, to think of the scenes that bring about a resolution. If you haven't seen the movie yet, it will be of value to you in understanding synchronicity through a life study. If you are skeptical of this concept, it may make more sense to think of the instances of synchronicity in your own life as a chain of events in the whole picture of your life, not just as links that happened here and there.

I would like to put forward an analogy as a way to understand synchronicity. In motion pictures, actors and actresses are cast into roles that they take on and develop. Some of the actors are "typecast" and we may see them in several movies in the same kinds of roles, or in Jungian terms, *archetypes*. These could be roles that are familiar to us: the villain, the mother, the good guy in the white hat, the innocent. Archetypes are as varied as the roles that are played in life. In fact, one way to think of archetypes is that they are metaphors for personality characteristics. If we are describing someone who just joined our team at work, we can say, "he's a villain" or "she's a dutiful daughter," and we are quick to understand this person in a general sense.

I will be describing synchronicity in terms of four roles that it can assume—typecasting it, as it were. Instead of roles that characters would play, I've grouped together aspects of synchronicity that fit into four general areas: Recognition, Warning, Revelation, and Verification. These four areas were chosen because of the benefits they can give to entrepreneurs while problem solving.

Let's delve into these areas through stories to discuss how these types are applied and how they affect entrepreneurs by making us more aware and able to satisfy human needs.

RECOGNITION

This is when synchronicity leads to a valuable discovery. The corresponding voice says "Aha!" "Eureka!" or "That's the answer!" You feel a combination of surprise and satisfaction upon finding an answer to your concern or problem. The benefit of recognition events is that they give us the resources and ideas we need to make decisions. They make us think. If we are sitting at our desk thinking about ways to sell a unique product, one from the product line not announced yet, and someone brings in an idea without prompting or knowing you were even looking at this product idea, that would be a recognition event.

As an entrepreneur, in the recognition area I want to be able to recognize opportunities, to pursue the ideas and information to help a client or create a business. Sometimes recognition gives me a jolt, shocks me, but it satisfies a human need in giving me the answer or a way to find the answer I am looking for, and the benefit is that it gives me the resources and ideas to make decisions.

George Akers is the creator of O Wear in Los Angeles, a manufacturer of "green cotton" sportswear. *Green cotton* refers to a specific method of growing and processing cotton. The cotton is organic, grown without pesticides, and processed without bleaching, creating a natural color with a hint of beige. George tells us how he credits synchronicity in his success: "These events have been the turning point in creating every product or company I have ever been involved in. For example, in 1989 I was in the process of exploring a 'life change.' I knew I did not necessarily want to leave the clothing industry, but I was sure I did not want to continue to pursue it in my current circumstance of being a sales representative. I went to London that fall, and by chance I happened to spot in a shop window a shirt made from green cotton. That was to be the pivotal event in my forming O Wear, America's first 100 percent organic cotton clothing company, because I reasoned that if you could make clothes the 'green' way, you could also probably grow the cotton they were made from a purer, safer way. The rest, as they say, is history."

George did not expect to find the answer to his vocational dilemma through a store display. But upon seeing that shirt, something clicked inside, a possibility for a business engaged.

Searching for an opportunity, George was looking for signs or options that might fall into place for his life change.

WARNING

Synchronistic events can play a role in warning us of situations or decisions we should approach with caution. Warning is characterized by an "uh-oh" voice. Warnings protect our bodies and our well-being. They protect our families, our companies, our interests and ideas. An example would be interviewing a person for a position, and hearing something inside telling you to look further, to ask for more references, or to ask the person back for a second interview with another staff member.

The warning type of synchronicity protects us. We want to be warned, to know if something is not in our best interest or if there are elements of a contract or project that we need to consider further. For example, if I am ready to sign a contract, I could synchronistically meet a person who has experience with the company I am considering. What they tell me may affect my decision, and in turn I will be more successful in the different aspects of the job, or, I may decide not to take the contract.

This type of synchronistic experience can give us clues to make a decision or to be aware of the consequences of a decision. Entrepreneur Greg Steltenpohl, founder of Odwalla Inc., a manufacturer and distributor of delicious natural juices, uses synchronistic experiences while decision making in this way: "I look for the unique quality of the experience—its resonance. For example, hearing the sickening crunch of metal when a driver backs into a parked car, while considering moving ahead on a project might suggest not moving ahead or proceeding with extreme caution." Steltenpohl also remarked that "a sonorous bell chiming at the moment of someone's suggestion might make me take it into special consideration, or add to the impulse of going forward. I have sometimes used a loud pop from logs in the fireplace at the moment of a certain thought as either caution or encouragement regarding a particular deliberation."

REVELATION

"Hmmm . . . ," could be the reaction to a new information-type synchronistic experience. These events give us new information about a person or situation. With recognition, synchronicity is more of a flash that happens within a shorter period of time. With revelation, the information comes first, and the synchronicity is revealed at a later time. It is less of a surprise than recognition, but it is stored, pondered on for later use. Revelation experiences can be motivators, creating links we can look to for further affirmation. An example of this would be reading the paper about something that grabs your attention, like a profile of a person, in a section of the paper you do not normally read. Later you meet this person at a meeting and you will be able to solve a problem because of this person's input.

People read newspapers and journals and talk with other people to gather information that may be of value to them later. In the revelation area, I want to be able to read the trends going on in the world. Synchronistic events can alert me to a trend or something of significance that can affect me in the future. It meets the human need of motivating me by creating this synchronistic experience in paths I could follow. Related to the recognition type of synchronicity, revelation goes deeper. It gives more information, information that may not be immediately discernible.

Anthropology was the subject of a series of events that occurred within two days in my life. This subject is not one I normally think about during the day in a conscious manner. The series of events started during a phone conversation with a colleague. She told me she was taking an anthropology class. Later that day a friend called, saying an acquaintance was taking an anthropology class, and did I ever consider being an anthropologist? That evening, a third friend gave me a book by anthropologist Mary Leaky, without my having said anything about the other two conversations. As the last event, I received a birthday card early the next day from my brother, with the greeting, "Happy Birthday, you old fossil," and at that moment I remembered that I share my birthday with anthropologist Margaret Mead.

In the inner world, I pondered the meaning of these occurrences at the time, wondering what it all meant. I remembered Jung's series of experiences with either real fish or fish symbols. In one day he had nine encounters having to do with fish: a client brought in a drawing, someone mentioned an "April Fish," and even while he was documenting in his journal the series of the fish occurrences, he looked down to see a fish at his feet!

In the outer world, I was working with a client who was a challenging experience. We hit a particularly rough time the next week during a strategic planning session, when people were split into groups of differing opinions on ways to pursue the future. One of the evenings I spent considering the series of events around anthropology, and the next day, used the theme of anthropology to work through notions and norms that the group was stuck in to consolidate and encourage them to move forward. We had to get through the first conflict, one of territory. We explored the cultures that did not have private property protected by fence posts and security devices. What did gaining or losing territory mean? Did it mean a gain or loss in power? of face? a loss of resources to gain capital? I asked them to consider sharing resources as a first step, looking at how threatening it would be to each person gathered. To some, sharing resources did mean a loss of prestige, of power. They would lose their standing, their corner office, their parking space. To some, sharing intellectual resources meant never getting the credit for their ideas. When all of these real issues were out on the table, we realized that the conflict was a cry for understanding. We moved on to the next part of our meetings, the real reason why we were there.

Revelation experience is different from the recognition type of synchronicity because it does not give a directive on the way to solve a problem at the moment. It is more subtle, giving us something to ponder until it is useful in decision making, or as in the case above, working toward conflict resolution.

VERIFICATION

The last type of synchronicity is titled verification. Verification is a feeling of being validated for following a path that doesn't make sense or a decision that did not follow the usual order. An "Ahh!" of relief, or "Yes!" as a sign of affirmation could be two of the responses. The benefit of a verification type of experience is that it can comfort and console. It gives us feedback that the decisions we have made are right for us. An example here would be a person making the decision to quit a regular, full-time paying job to create his or her own business. The next day after the decision, someone calls not knowing the decision has been made and eventually becomes the first client.

We have all been in situations where others thought we were crazy or making a big mistake with our business. "You'll never make it" or "that's really a brainless idea" may be what we tell ourselves or hear from other people. People said to Ray Kinsella in *Field of Dreams*, "Why did you plow under your corn? Especially to make a baseball field with no team! You will lose your farm." We hear these voices from other people while our internal voices tell us to go ahead with our plans. The verification type of synchronicity gives entrepreneurs affirmation and assurance that their choices, however crazy they may be to others, have been correct for them. When we receive a verification, it means that the path we have chosen, have formulated within the interior world, has been validated by the external world.

Jackie Sa, the Mill Valley, California, founder of Tea Garden Springs spa told me:

> It was one of those life-changing experiences. I just closed a business that I had been doing for two years which I didn't find a soulful satisfaction from. I just "paused" and wondered what I wanted to do with my life. I was sitting and daydreaming in front of the Palace of Fine Art in San Francisco with my good friend Cyndy, and expressing out loud an idea that I had not thought of before—I wanted to create a Chinese herbal shop, a unique one and not like the ones in San Francisco's Chinatown,

to introduce Chinese herbal food therapy to the Western people who are not familiar with this profound, yet balanced way of living and maintaining health. This is my way of life, coming from three generations of an herbal family. I told Cyndy that I would plunge ahead and create this unique store that had no precedence anywhere, on the following conditions being met: It had to be (1) in Mill Valley (at the time, I knew nothing about Mill Valley—I was a San Francisco girl); (2) a certain square footage; (3) the maximum rent that I could afford; and (4) the landlord or leasing company had to agree to just a one-year lease in case my "crazy" concept didn't work (all commercial leases are generally stipulated at three to five years, minimum). Cyndy was clearly puzzled. Why had I specified Mill Valley? I'd been there only once for dinner and had never even seen the town! The next day she, her husband, and I hopped in the car and drove to Mill Valley to explore. Three days and several phone calls later, I found my perfect location for the store (right in the heart of downtown Mill Valley). It met every one of my above conditions to a "T"! I was stunned. Before I knew it, I'd signed the lease and put into motion an herbal store without any prior knowledge of sourcing, business plans, etc. That was in 1991, and since then, wondrous synchronicities keep on happening . . .

Jackie's intent was clear, and her stipulations certain. Although she was stunned that her dream could be a reality in just three days, she went ahead with her business. Jackie found that it was essential to say what she wanted out loud and with intention. At the time when she stated what she wanted, she didn't worry about whether or not she had enough money, was worthy of creating this, or if Mill Valley would have the clientele that would be interested in what she had to offer. She had the drive coupled with faith to make it successful. Jackie was aware that she was going against the odds, trying to find a location that would be the right one. She depended upon her business sense and experience to have Plan B (what if this crazy idea doesn't work?). These events of synchronicity verified Jackie's desires to own a business, her conditions for being in business, and her desire to provide a service that would be healing to her clientele.

Echoing Jackie's experience, Elliot Hoffman, entrepreneur of Just Desserts, a San Francisco bakery, tells how, at a critical growing point in his company, he was aware of synchronicity. Instead of telling someone his needs out loud, he found that writing his needs on a card with the same intent was the method that worked for him. He recalled a specific instance when it helped to create a location he wanted.

> I was looking for a new facility and I wrote down how much square footage I would need, what freeways it needed to be close to, and even the specific brand of refrigeration units. The next day, a vendor hands me a card with an available rental— the location fit my requirements almost exactly, right down to the brand name refrigeration units that I wanted!

Another story about finding the location that made a restaurant a success comes from David Foeke, creator of Cafe Flora, located in Seattle's Madison Park neighborhood. David talked about the series of events that led to the opening of his restaurant by reflecting on intuitive feelings and acting on them.

> I had an intuitive sense of the need to call immediately about the For Sale sign on the building we eventually purchased for our restaurant. Sure enough, on that day an offer was being delivered by another party. We happened to be in a certain location on the East Coast for a three-hour period during which a critical phone call arrived to allow the purchase of our building.

David credits his success to his intuition and awareness of synchronicity. "[If I had not been listening to my intuition], we would definitely not have the location we have. This has been critical for our success . . . it was clearly opportune for us. We had a line out the door with a full house the first weekend, in spite of no advertising."

The last story in this area of verification has a different twist, and it has to do with synchronicity happening when working with clients who refuse your idea, and make you feel like the cards are stacked against you. This example comes from Kathy Gardarian, founder of Qualis International, a leader in recycled plastic bag manufacturing. "I recall one time I was negotiating with a buyer in his office in another state, and he was disagreeing with me that a certain program would work. In the middle of the meeting, the president of the company called my buyer to specifically mention my name and how much he liked the program. He didn't even know I was in town, sitting in the buyer's office!"

Kathy's story is truly remarkable isn't it? Imagine being in a situation of not being able to make progress with a prospective customer, only to have the president of the buyer's firm call on your behalf, without your knowledge? What would you think if you were Kathy? Then again, what would you think if you were the buyer?

A story like this makes us realize how much we need to follow through with the awareness of our synchronicities, or the messages that synchronicity tells us. We may decide to follow those messages, even though it seems like a crazy idea, as it did to Jackie Sa. Our journey may be to drive cross-country like Ray Kinsella or to start a business like George Akers did.

We've explored synchronicity through different angles. In Chapter 1 we looked at synchronicity through definitions, historical stories, and from the view of several entrepreneurs. The second chapter gave us perspective on synchronicity through life situations that are common to us all, time periods of intense personal change: falling in love, exploring roots, and crisis situations. The third chapter provides a framework to understand these experiences through four areas that benefit the entrepreneur and to engage in a creative and successful business.

QUESTIONS

Considering the four areas of "Typecasting Synchronicity" have you:

1. Recognized occasions that an answer or solution you were looking for appeared?
2. Had times when a synchronistic event or events pointed out something to warn you to act or not act a certain way?
3. Had events happen over a period of time that gelled together to form situations that helped you at the right time?
4. Experienced synchronistic events that verified a decision you made or acknowledged a chosen path where you wanted to go?
5. Are there times you have heard a voice, as Ray Kinsella did with "Build it and they will come," and followed that voice?

Different internal and external voices come to us during our lifetimes. The "devil's advocate" voices, those questioning voices that ask, "What are you talking about? Are you crazy?" can be valuable to you, as can the directive voice saying "build it and they will come."

Questions like those above have been valuable to me in consulting with groups. When I work with some teams, people can be skeptical: "this sounds like another lame idea," or "we did something like this three years ago and it didn't work, so what makes you think it will work now?"

I had the opportunity to work with a group when one of the sponsors tried to kick a person off the team early in the project. She was a bright, competent, idealistic person who stuck her opinion in at every opportunity. This really irritated the sponsor. I knew intuitively that she would be one of the most valuable people in the group, and I persuaded the sponsor not to take her off the project just yet. By the end of the phase it was clear to all that she was an essential part of the team, and saved us from our worst mistakes.

Chapter 4

Who Are Entrepreneurs, Anyway?

Walking down the hall one spring evening, rounding the corner into a classroom, I overheard a comment a second-year MBA student in finance made to a prospective student: "Oh yeah, in this classroom are the entrepreneurship students. They are really confused and a bunch of dreamers, and lust after other people's money. You don't want to do that, do you?"

I was shocked. As an MBA student, with an entrepreneur emphasis, I had some idea of the observations and sometimes objections that people make about entrepreneurs, but I didn't realize it had reached the recruiting stages! Yet, perceptions of wanna-be entrepreneurs as an insecure and unstable lot persist. Paul Hawken reminds us from his personal experience: "A few weeks after I opened my store in Boston a friend asked pointblank, 'How does it feel to be an entrepreneur?' I was humiliated. Entrepreneurs were folks who sold T-shirts during papal visits or bottled water after natural disasters . . . I suddenly realized why my father, a photographer, and my mother, a research assistant, had not been jubilant at my decision to open a store, and wouldn't even tell their friends what I was doing . . .

They weren't the only people who flinched at my decision to enter business. Former teachers struggled to maintain a calm expression when I told them I was a storekeeper, friends expressed concern about my 'direction in life,' and old girlfriends didn't return my calls."[1]

Clarifying the entrepreneur's role is the purpose of this chapter. Those of you who are entrepreneurs will be able to identify with the situations and stories. Those of you who want to be entrepreneurs can study how you might fit into this entrepreneurial picture. Those of you with no entrepreneurial aspirations, especially those who are partners or companions of entrepreneurs, will gain an understanding of the entrepreneurial mindset.

As an entrepreneur, you may have heard one or more of the following questions:

"Why don't you get a real job, one that has some stability and a future, instead of just dreaming?"

"You've got a family to think about now. You need to start thinking of things other than that crazy idea of yours!"

"Are you going to keep changing jobs every two years? Can't you just stick it out a few more years? What's the matter with you?"

If you know an entrepreneur, you may have asked the same questions, or have thought "Just who do they think they are, anyway?"

JUST WHO ARE ENTREPRENEURS ANYWAY?

An entrepreneur once remarked that all of those in business for themselves made a courageous decision. And we see the evidence of successful entrepreneurs in everyday life; most businesses began with a "crazy idea." Aircraft were once seen as bizarre contraptions without any future in the commercial world, even after the Wright brothers proved flight was possible.

---

1. Paul Hawken, *Growing a Business* (New York: Simon & Schuster, 1987) 16–17.

It took an entrepreneur to turn the contraptions into an industry: William Boeing, who in 1916 created Pacific Aero Products, later to become The Boeing Company. At the time, Boeing kept his vision alive and pursued the future in flight, not only to transport mail and cargo, but to take people from one place to another. Automobiles, also thought at one time not to have a future, had an entrepreneur in Henry Ford.

Entrepreneurs are described in many ways. *Webster's* defined an entrepreneur as "one who organizes and directs a business undertaking, assuming the risk for the sake of the profit."[2] G.T. Solomon said that the "entrepreneur's challenge was to find and use new ideals to jostle the economy out of an otherwise repetitive cycle of activities. . . . They were creators of new business combinations."[3] Martin Krieger refers to entrepreneurs as "creative destroyers."[4]

The entrepreneurs I have talked with or read about also expanded the definition. Devi Jacobs, founder of Outback, a clothing retailer in Berkeley, California, has gems of wisdom, "Sometimes people go into business to follow an idea, but not themselves. Sometimes it is a good idea, but it is not who they are." She recommends, "Find who you are, the seeds are there. Things will unfold and blossom," and Paul Hawken echoes, "It's a way to become who you are."[5]

The entrepreneurial spirit is a creative force in a person who combines ideas, action, and actuality. To exclude any of the three dimensions would make an entrepreneur not be an entrepreneur. People wonder whether or not entrepreneurs' skills and aptitudes are innate or fostered, a product of nature or nurture. I believe it is developed both ways. It is not an either/or but a both/and situation, and perhaps even more than a both/and. Articles in popular magazines about entrepreneurship, some

2. N. Webster, *Webster's New Twentieth Century Dictionary of the English Language, Second Edition* (San Francisco: Collins World, 1975) 608.

3. Bruce Whiting and George Solomon, *Key Issues in Creativity, Innovation, and Entrepreneurship* (Buffalo: Bearly Limited, 1989) 28.

4. Martin Krieger, *Entrepreneurial Vocations* (Atlanta: Scholar's Press, 1996) 91.

5. Paul Hawken, *Growing a Business* (New York: Simon & Schuster, 1987) 19.

with quizzes, such as, "Are You an Entrepreneur?: Test Your-self," usually contain questions that have elements of both. The important thing is that you recognize the entrepreneur in yourself. The quizzes may give you a starting point, as will friends and mentors who will encourage and support you and give feedback about your ability, but your beliefs are the key.

You most likely know people who have entered into acting, perhaps taking a class or being an extra in a movie or stage production. They crave the next acting experience. We even have a phrase for it—"catching the acting bug." Entrepreneurs also feel the heady, sometimes compulsive calling to create a new business. Like acting, it is a way to use more of your skills and fill the role you were meant to play.

Some people speculate that the entrepreneur's desire to be in business is based on the need to prove something, that a business is a way to push self-development and self-esteem. That is only part of the story. I believe there are also other factors, philanthropic ones: the desire to make the future of our planet more inhabitable, social benefits, and an emphasis on seeing more than just the financial bottom line. Business is a means of providing the fuel, the drive for the entrepreneur.

If the entrepreneur is the engine that runs the business, ideas are the entrepreneur's battery, where energy is created and stored. This is where the entrepreneur reads the trends, talks with people, and catches the hunches that formulate business opportunities. The next dimension is action, promoting the ideas, testing the market, and educating people about the benefits of the product or service offered. In action, entrepreneurs are not only looking at developing skills in marketing, manufacturing, service, and finance, but also developing qualities in themselves, characteristics we will be looking at in depth in Part II. To complete the circle, making things real, or actuality, is necessary for an entrepreneur. This involves the steps of securing capital, marketing, and making the actual product or performing the actual service.

To elaborate on entrepreneurs, I've chosen three roles they play. We may see entrepreneurs as artists (the creators of vision), articulators (conveyors of need), and alchemists (the manifestors). These generalizations are helpful in discussing the roles of entrepreneurs, and are not to be seen as a step-by-step process but to be recognized as interacting with each other, as part of a web.

CREATORS OF VISION: ENTREPRENEURS AS ARTISTS

Norman Maclean, author of *A River Runs Through It*, once commented: "One of my fascinations about my own life is that every now and then I see a thing that unravels as if an artist had made it. It has a beautiful design and shape and rhythm."[6] This can be true of creating businesses. While some might disagree that this quote is applicable for the start-up phase of business, most would agree that the vision is the ideal, the place where you want to be, the company you want to create, and the customers you want to serve. The entrepreneur will elaborate on the vision, and later will need the help of others to focus the ideas into frames of priorities and goals to achieve his or her mission.

Beautiful rhythms can come from a jazz ensemble. In *The Creative Spirit*, musician Benny Golson is interviewed about collaboration. "First of all, collaboration is a matter of choice. But once the choice is made, it is made because those two or three or more people who are collaborating believe in one another. But then once you do, it is very much like iron sharpening iron. When you rub two pieces together they refine each other. You tend to fill in the gaps that the other didn't consider. One person becomes a barometer for the other. And one person encourages the other."[7]

6. Nicholas O'Connell, *At Field's End* (Seattle: Madrona, 1987) 193.

7. David Goleman, Paul Kaufman, and Michael Ray, *The Creative Spirit* (New York: Plume, 1992) 121.

As I work with entrepreneurs in my consulting business, I use familiar metaphors to develop and explain certain points. Metaphors are ways of understanding and integrating new ideas from a comparison with something already known. They can streamline and make something understandable quickly. If we are already familiar with something like a sport used as a metaphor, we can quickly assimilate what a person is trying to convey. The disadvantage of metaphors is that they can be tired and overused and they can separate us if we are offended by them, or they don't suit our values. Some do not translate into other languages and cultures. Types of metaphors that are familiar to us are: sports analogies about *team* and *playing fields*; military analogies using words such as *battle, war,* and *enemy*; game metaphors include phrases like *it's a deal, putting all your cards on the table,* and *playing (or not playing) with a full deck*; and of course, there's always the overworked *apples* and *oranges* metaphor.

Joseph Jaworski, author of *Synchronicity: The Inner Path of Leadership*, recalls an experience in using metaphors at a meeting of Shell Corporation in South Africa. They used birds to label the four scenarios they were looking at for the future of the corporation and the country. In the "ostrich" scenario, the government "sticks its head in the sand" and does not pursue free election. "Lame duck" was the second scenario which, in Joe's words, "is what might happen in a prolonged transition . . . the government purports to respond to all, but satisfies none." The third scenario, "Icarus," would "try to satisfy all the promises made during the campaign . . . embark on a huge, unsustainable spending program and consequently crash the economy." The final scenario was "flamingos." It was "chosen because when flamingos fly, they rise slowly, but they fly together. In this scenario, improvement is gradual and—most important—participatory."[8] The use of birds illustrated the scenarios well, as the characteristics of the chosen birds reflected meaningfully to the participants the action of each scenario.

8. Joseph Jaworski, *Synchronicity: The Inner Path of Leadership* (Berkeley, CA: Berrett-Koehler, 1996) 162–163.

I choose art metaphors when I work with entrepreneurs. The reasons are twofold: one, is that it is unique and meaningful, and the second is that since many of them have either studied art or have a deep appreciation of it, they are valuable to them.

I introduce what is known as the *elements* of art. A student of art learns about the elements or qualities essential to a work of art—a painting, sculpture, a costume. As in the last chapter, where we cast synchronistic experiences together so we could understand these events better, the elements of art can form groups to create an entrepreneurial "work of art" and apply it to the workplace. For example, *unity* as an element serves the purpose of making all the parts of a painting reflect a whole, or a common theme. The element of *balance* gives us a sense of continuity, that a sculpture is not too heavy on one side or another. *Repetition*, like the multiple use of the same words or rhythm in a poem, reiterates a point. *Color* gives us more information about a piece of art, creates mood, excites, and captures our attention.

For the first element, unity, I ask entrepreneurs how they think their idea of a business can be translated into viable plans. Are the ideas inside the entrepreneur's mind consistent with what they can accomplish? Do they coincide with values they hold close? Are they the right match for the idea they want to promote, based on their temperament and who they are?

Answers or comments brought up during the discussion vary. Sometimes people I talk with do not want to take an entrepreneurial path after discussing how disunifying it might be in their life. They see it as too much risk, that not having a consistent flow of money will disrupt their lives, or that they do not have the time and energy to become fluent in the language of business. Others are not entrepreneurs because they do not have the drive, desire, or ability to ask questions and to seek common goals with other people.

Conversely, some are even more convinced they are entrepreneurs. They see entrepreneurship as a way of using more of their abilities, keeping congruence of values between their personal and business life, and positively affecting the future. A woman considering expanding her copy and printing shop was at a crossroads and not able to explain where she wanted to go. I asked her, "What is it you really want to do?" and without hesitation, she replied, "I want to go back to school and become a nutritionist." We explored the unity of her life. Could she expand her business and still go to school? No. Could she go back to school, keeping interest in the shop? No. Would she really like to sell or close her shop and return to school? Yes. So steps were taken in that direction. No doubt she would have been a success had she kept her shop; she was a competent, creative, caring individual. But looking at the unity of her life and her goals in the larger picture, going back to school was the best choice for her.

For the second element, balance, I ask, "Does the idea you hold balance with what resources are at your disposal? Is this idea in balance with what you want in your life? What about the responsibilities (family, home, other employment, and community activities) that you already hold? Can you balance your dream with the needs of those who depend on you? Are you able to balance your own life in a healthy way, turning your mind off when it is time to sleep?"

Balance seems to be one of the most difficult areas in life, and no person I've ever worked with in business has managed it consistently. I've asked several people whom I have worked with over the years about this—a general, a governor, several middle managers, executives, and entrepreneurs in all fields—some have felt the frustration of not having enough time with their family and friends, not taking care of their health the way they would like.

Sometimes entrepreneurs go into business because of their desire not to work traditional hours. Yvon Chouinard, founder of Patagonia, an active sportswear company, remarked "I have become a businessman whether I wanted to admit it or not, but I decided that if I was going to stick with it, I was going to do it on my own terms . . . [I] didn't have to go nine to five. If the surf was up I could take off and go surfing anytime."[9]

9. David Goleman, Paul Kaufman, and Michael Ray, *The Creative Spirit* (New York: Plume 1992) 66, 140–141.

For the third element, repetition, I ask if they are consistent in repeating the message of their business to their associates, stockholders, vendors, the community, and other stakeholders. Are their mission and their values consistent with every aspect of their business?

Discussion around the element of repetition focuses on the messages, blatant or subtle, that affect the success of the company. People I have worked with wonder what their customers are thinking, and are sometimes hesitant to ask. Others ask all the time.

Repetition looks at the mission of the company, and one of the most valuable exercises is completing a "mission statement match." Look at it both quantitatively and qualitatively. Quantitative evaluation includes looking at the hard numbers; for example, take each value that your statement says you hold dear and see how it looks next to the balance sheet. How are you spending your money? Do you spend it on what you want your company to be? Also look at the qualitative side, which looks at areas that are less easy to put into numbers, but are just as important. Are your customers happy with your company? How about your employees? Many entrepreneurs I've assisted through this exercise are surprised to see the evidence of their support, or lack thereof, of the mission statement and the way money is spent.

For the metaphor of color, I ask, "Do your ideas give you energy, or does even thinking of them overwhelm or drag you down? Do you have enough interest and energy in your ideas to educate, explain, and give numerous presentations to various people? Are your ideas exciting enough to provide the stamina you need to make them become real? What colors do you associate with your ideas? vibrant orange? pale blue? a subtle brown?

Color is such a fun and wonderful element to inspire people. Color represents so many things to us. When we are unhappy there is a "black cloud over our heads," and when we feel depressed we are "feeling blue." One important thing to note is that different colors have different meanings to different people. Red can mean action to some, caution to others. Blue can mean depression for some, or blue skies to others—as in the problem I had is clearing, and I now have a solution.

If you are laughing because you think this is a silly idea, you would be amazed by the usefulness of color as a metaphor. For example, while an entrepreneur is explaining a problem and seems to be at an impasse, I ask them what color they see. Do they see red? or black? It gives me clues about where to take the conversation from there.

Metaphors are an effective tool used to educate and convey your point quickly. They are best understood when you select analogies that are familiar to you and to those you educate, and are appropriate to the situation. Metaphors that are increasing in use are ones to do with nature, like in the idea of *flow* of a stream or river or interconnectivity, "the Web"; *electricity* with words such as "spark," in the term "the spark of an idea." Metaphors change over time, so it is important that they be chosen wisely; if they are not, you will lose your point and your audience.

CONVEYERS OF NEED: ENTREPRENEURS AS ARTICULATORS

Sam Hill, a quintessential entrepreneur, was the son-in-law of J. J. Hill, the railroad tycoon. Although Sam spent time in Minnesota with his father-in-law, he also had a law practice during the late 19th and early 20th century. Not only did Sam participate in a law practice, but he also tried to start a Quaker community, build monuments, and operated a telephone company. During Sam's lifetime, one of his areas of special interest was the creation of roadway networks. At a time when automobile roads were built poorly and inconsistently, and freeways and highway systems were nonexistent, this colorful man lectured and promoted good roads not only in the United States, but also overseas. Hill the entrepreneur felt so strongly about his vision that he said, "Good roads are my religion."

Hill's vision was simply this: good roads to be able to transport people and things from one place to another. This was in the early 1900s. At that time, people didn't see the need for roads, and didn't see the impact that the automobile would have on their way of life. He traveled widely, networking with important decision makers, articulating the need he saw as crucial to his success. He knew that having good roads would connect people, products, and information. Just think of what people would have thought about good roads then: Isn't the railroad good enough? rivers? trails? Consider for a moment the view at the time that railroads and rivers were the way people and products were transported.

Sam Hill remarked to J. J. Hill "You told me once, Mr. Hill, that a railroad without terminals was like a body without arms and legs . . . you forget that you need more than arms and legs for your railroad systems; you must have toes and fingers to reach . . . the farm." Sam also told author Fred Lockley that he also said to Hill, "I am going to see a highway built through British Columbia down our own coastline, clear to Mexico and it's going to be a hard-surfaced road." In 1929 he added, "302,000 autos crossed the borderline at Blaine [Washington State, near Vancouver, British Columbia] and they carried over a million passengers."[10]

This articulation, partnered with the conviction that Sam Hill clearly used, means strengthening one's viewpoint and thought clearly to reach beyond the present and connect people to the future. There are many examples of products that we now take for granted that were considered exotic at one time: personal computers, coffee, White Out, and Post-It Notes. Guy Kawasaki, a marketing consultant, formerly of Apple computer, explains the elements of evangelical marketing in his book, *Selling the Dream*. Another grand articulator is Howard Schultz, CEO of Starbucks Coffee company. As a speaker, he promotes

10. John E. Tuhy, *Sam Hill, The Prince of Castle Nowhere* (Portland, OR: Timber Press, 1993) 130.

coffee with passion, educating us to the possibilities of a great cup of coffee. Remember when we bought coffee in a can at the grocery store, and at a restaurant, simply asked for "coffee." Now we can buy coffee from a coffee retailer and ask for coffee from a barista using multiple adjectives: "I want a single, tall, skinny, latte," for example.

MANIFESTING: ENTREPRENEURS AS ALCHEMISTS

Alchemists were people who blended elements together in their search for ways to make other elements, especially gold. They were people with a desire to heal and to prolong life. I see entrepreneurs as alchemists because they take many elements of energy in the forms of people, capital, computers, machinery, and transportation and put them together to manifest, or make into reality, a business.

When people think of manifestation, they might recall a biblical story about receiving manna in the desert, when no food was to be seen anywhere. How did something come from what seemed to be nothing? I also take the latter part of the word and think of feasting as in *festival* and *feast*. Manifesting well includes an element of joy. Entrepreneurship should have that element in it. I recall a story about Ben and Jerry of Ben & Jerry's Homemade, Inc., stressing that joy is an essential part of the entrepreneurial process. If it is not fun, then why take it upon yourself? If you can work for yourself and have fun, do it; otherwise, why not just work for someone else?

Entrepreneurs must figure out what they actually want and articulate it to themselves and others; *then* the manifestation starts occurring. People are attracted to what you are doing and the passion and energy you exude. Add a spark of interest and they become customers, employees, investors. We have to be clear in what we want and be able to accept the outcome, since things, including businesses, don't always go the way we plan them.

David Spangler, a prolific writer and past director of the Findhorn community in Scotland, recalled two stories about manifestation that illustrate how the interior mind reflects in the outer world. In one instance, Spangler was driving down the road. He recalls thinking, "I am so angry, I could smash glass," and in that instant, a rock went through his windshield. Another time, he had a clear prompting to call a hobby store while he was driving. He stopped at a pay phone, lifted the receiver to dial, and noticed that the line was already connected—to the exact store he wanted to call![11]

It may seem very farfetched or unlikely that these things occurred in that short a time, but that is what synchronicity is— the materialization of things that we carry in our minds appearing, at times apparently, out of nowhere. It baffles us because we are left to wonder how much control we really have over our lives. To explore this further, in Part II of this book I will introduce a phenomenon called the "24-hour window" that gives examples of entrepreneurs acting on their ideas within 24 hours of the idea's inception, and how they manifest what they want in a short period of time.

Contrary to the opinions of some, entrepreneurs are hardworking and thinking people who not only envision a solution to a problem or need but are capable of articulating this solution to others, to educate and motivate people. Through their contacts, problem-solving skills, and determination they can make those solutions manifest, bringing their visions into fruition.

Entrepreneurs cannot turn their spirit on or off. Their drive is an intrinsic part of who they are, and runs all day (and sometimes all night) long. Because they envision the future, they are seen as a bunch of dreamers. The inner drive to create something that uses their whole selves is something entrepreneurs know and deal with on a daily basis. This belies the idea that entrepre-

---

11. David Spangler, *Everyday Miracles: The Inner Art of Manifestation* (New York: Bantam, 1996) 63, 71.

neurs are not grounded in day-to-day life—if they were not a part of wise decision making and living in the moment, they would not be in business. To ride the tide of criticism, entrepreneurs have to have the inner drive to outweigh the adversarial comments that people can make. The entrepreneurial spirit can be spread and mentored. It is part of the artistry, articulation, and alchemy of entrepreneurship.

QUESTIONS TO ASK YOURSELF

1. Do you have a burning desire to be in business?
2. Are you dissatisfied that your current job only uses part of your skills?
3. Are you constantly looking for new ideas? Scanning newspapers and talking with people about the future?
4. Do you ever get an idea, think about it, let it go, and then find that in six months or a year someone else has developed the idea?
5. Do you talk with entrepreneurs?
6. Have you had a position that could be considered entrepreneurial in nature? Have you run for office, worked as an officer in a organization, been a minister in a religious or spiritual group, been an artist or musician?
7. Do you feel dissatisfied with the products you see on the market? Does your innovative mind work overtime going through catalogues, seeing how products could be made better?

Part II

Fire
The Action of Synchronicity

How can I be more aware of synchronicity?

To me, fire denotes action, an element that correlates with the driving force of synchronicity. This section of the book will outline six characteristics of entrepreneurs who are aware of and use synchronicity as a part of their business life. To put yourself in a frame of mind to read this part, consider the following questions and comments:

- In what ways am I already aware of synchronicity?
- What actions can I take to be more aware of synchronicity?
- What are my strengths in regard to personal qualities?
- What strengths lend themselves to being more aware of synchronicity?
- Do I consider myself an entrepreneur?
- Do I believe in intuition? How do I use it?
- How creative do I consider myself to be?

Chapter 5
Creation Through Intuition and Imagination

As a child, freshly awake before I was called to get up, I would lie on my back and take time to imagine what it would be like to live in the house upside down. What would it be like to step over the doorways, have the windows lower to the ground to light the hallway, and walk around light fixtures that glowed upwards instead of downwards?

What did you imagine as a child? That you would be traveling in flying machines from home to the store like Dick Tracy did, or transported from home to anywhere in the galaxy, beaming around like they did on *Star Trek*?

In this chapter, we'll explore the role creative thinking has on entrepreneurial minds. Two business partners are here to help us understand creative thinking: Imagination and Intuition. How does the entrepreneur's imagination work? How do they come up with ideas and innovations that they turn into a business? What goes on inside when they know they have decided what business they will start? In imagination we see the unique ways that entrepreneurs think, one of which is not following the status quo, the common path. There are four roles that intuition can play: inspiring muse, messenger of warning, coach, or dissatisfied voice.

IMAGINATION AS CREATIVE PARTNER

Imagination is a strong force, the way to use our talents and create things in the world. We see it clearly in children, in their spontaneity, their ways of solving problems. In many ways we laid the foundation of creativity by the games or activities we took time and energy to play when we were young. Listen to the way children perceive the world.

One day in the grocery store, I was introduced to a young girl. She asked, "What kind of Jessica *are* you?" I was puzzled and I asked her to explain. "Well, I'm the only April I know and I already know one Jessica, so what kind of Jessica are you?" I answered, "I'm Jessika who spells her name with a K." She nodded her head in acknowledgment, satisfied with my answer. At that age, the girl was learning to classify and organize her thoughts.

Ignoring the Status Quo   Entrepreneurs ignore the status quo. In seeing the world differently, they have the willingness to change, to lead and motivate people. For entrepreneurs who are reading this, you know how strong your feelings are toward your business and the improvements you can make for your customers and clients. You know the difference your business can make for social change in your community. You also know that it was somewhat difficult growing up in a society that doesn't value creative thinking. What happened when you were drawing, doodling, or looking out the window, envisioning other things during a lecture? When you decided to spell your name a unique way or to dress differently? Did you write letters to the editor or talk to people about something that was a common event, but that you thought could be done better.

A story of challenging the status quo in a big way comes from Anita Roddick: "When we did our recycling campaign, we printed 28 million bags for Body Shop products. Simple paper bags, all recycled. And we asked the government, "Why aren't you printing telephone bills and gas bills and electricity bills on recycled paper?" We put the idea on posters in our stores; we told the consumer how many millions we'd save each year, how many trees we'd save. And just to be cheeky—and this is an example of creativity at work—we also put the phone number or the address of the administrator to contact. They were bombarded with complaints! You just have to show people how they can do it, and it puts their thinking on another plane."[1]

An Idaho entrepreneur remarked in an interview, "I have my own show. I can plan, create my own resources, take care of my employees, and help the community. I could always work for someone else, but why should I if I can keep going?"

Imagination helps us create what is possible, helps us envision our future, reach our dreams. Imagining the future as it could be takes great risk. It takes being vulnerable to what ideas we may come up with. It takes shutting off any critical voices or thinking that would interrupt the flow of ideas. George Land and Beth Jarman's book, *Breakpoint and Beyond*, gives us an example of how the critical voice holds us back. George gave eight tests of divergent creative thinking to 1,600 children in the early days of the Headstart program. He gave the same tests to these children over several years. The first tests were given when the children were between three and five years of age. Ninety-eight percent of the children scored in the genius category. When these same children took identical tests five years later, only 32 percent scored that high. Five years later it was down to 10 percent. Two

---

1. David Goleman, Paul Kaufman, and Michael Ray, *The Creative Spirit* (New York: Plume, 1992) 123.

hundred thousand adults over the age of twenty-five have taken the same tests. Only 2 percent scored at the genius level. What happens?[2]

Land and Jarman explain that the socialization process restricts creative thinking because of our value judgments toward our thoughts and the opinions of others: "That's a bad idea," "Where did you get that idea," "That's stupid" are some of the critical voices we hear. Even more detrimental is when the opinion is personalized and becomes a part of what we think: "you're stupid" or "I must be stupid."

How can we reverse this trend that undermines creative thinking? We can't just toss socialization out the window or what would happen? Socialization is important. It teaches us how to act in situations, relate to people, and live in society. If the pendulum swings too far the other way, the result is chaos, indecision, and inaction.

It is imperative that we take a middle ground of valuing both socialization and imagination. An example comes from the book *Orbiting the Giant Hairball: A Corporate Fool's Guide to Surviving with Grace* by Gordon MacKenzie, veteran of Hallmark cards. Gordon is highly creative, working every ounce of creativity all the time. He spoke about how this negative voice in the guise of teasing destroys our creativity. He recalled a session he led about creativity, working with a group that did not want to share their ideas, causing him great frustration.

Gordon's frustration with this group reminds me of the story from Chapter 1 about the Golden Scarab. He must have felt what Jung felt in dealing with his patient, wondering where to go from here. However, Gordon found his "scarab" in a woman in the back of the room. She had an open look on her face, as if she wanted to share. He took the cue and asked, "Would you like to share something?" She said she would, and told her idea. The idea did not sit well with the rest of the group.

2. George Land and Beth Jarman, *Breakpoint and Beyond: Mastering the Future—Today* (New York: Harper Business, 1992) 153.

In fact, people started teasing her, attacking her for her idea. After MacKenzie stopped them, the whole group shifted into a discussion about teasing. Some people saw it as a way to show affection. By the end of the day people actually saw another story, the story of destruction of a person's self-worth and the creative connection.

The next partner in creativity is intuition. Intuition helps us make business and personal decisions, can give clues for action in our usual, daily thoughts, and some information that is critical that is not given to us by usual means.

INTUITION AS CREATIVE PARTNER

Ask yourself: Do I get signals throughout the day and feelings that tell me that something is going to happen? Is there something I need to be aware of? Is there a feeling somewhere in my body that tells me the truth about something or someone I might not be conscious of?

In creative thinking, intuition is an essential partner. Carol Frenier tells us, "Intuition gives us a holistic picture that comes from within; it is a gut feeling, as opposed to the data that we get directly through our senses of seeing, hearing, tasting, smelling, and touching."[3] Intuition is the feeling in our physical bodies that comes from more than just our traditional senses. "A sense for the unknowable and the ability to foresee the unforeseeable"[4] is the definition found early in Robert Greenleaf's *Servant Leadership*. How can we attune to this ability? Peter Senge correlates intuition and reason using the analogy of nature designing in pairs. "Two legs are critical for rapid, flexible locomotion. Two arms are vital for climbing, lifting, and manipulating objects. Two eyes give us stereoscopic vision, and along with two ears, depth perception. Is it not possible that, following the same

3. Carol Frenier, *Business and the Feminine Principle: The Untapped Resource* (Boston: Butterworth-Heinemann, 1997) 23.

4. Robert Greenleaf, *Servant Leadership: A Journey Into the Nature of Legitimate Power and Greatness* (Boston: Little, Brown, 1986) 22.

design principle, reason and intuition are designed to work in harmony for us to achieve our potential intelligence?"[5] I agree with Senge that we need both reason and intuition, striking a balance between the extremes of either one.

Entrepreneurs talk about intuition as an "inner trust," "gut feeling," or "inner voice." Intuition is the source of inspiration, the whisper that benefits your growth. It can come in the forms of the inspiring muse, a messenger of warning, a coach, or a dissatisfied voice.

The *inspiring muse* role of intuition is what we hear about in artistic realms: the inspiration to paint, to write, to sculpt. It can also occur in a business sense: the hint to call someone now, to buy a stock, to finish a proposal today instead of tomorrow. For instance, in the middle of a meeting someone makes a suggestion that inspires you to make a phone call. You don't know exactly if the idea will work, or if you will be criticized for it, but you feel very compelled to do it anyway. I have been in the middle of a meeting when someone mentioned a conference the next month in another city, concerning issues not related to leadership, entrepreneurship, or topics that are related to the workshops I usually give. Though I had a full schedule, something inspired me to find out more about this conference, and I was able to present a workshop there which influenced and benefited the attendees.

Mary Kay Ash describes an example of how the *messenger of warning* worked in her favor when starting Mary Kay Cosmetics in 1963. Her staff consisted of nine people—eight inexperienced people and one man who "sounded like a marketing whiz . . . I had already promised to hire him." However, after spending more time talking to him, she changed her mind. "I had no reason, just intuition. Six months later I read in the newspaper that he had been indicted on a felony."[6] The intuitive messenger of warning let her know something was not right, and she followed through with that voice.

5. Peter Senge, *The Fifth Discipline* (New York: Doubleday, 1990) 168.
6. Roy Rowan, *The Intuitive Manager* (Boston: Little, Brown, 1986) 17.

The *coach* gives us encouragement when we are in need of consolation or cheerleading. It tells us to move on, to believe in ourselves, in our vision, to continue on course and trust ourselves. Ah!laska entrepreneur Donna Maltz says that her decisions are based on inner trust: "I have an attitude about decision making. I make it, and I trust myself that it is the best decision I can make." Inner trust is directly related to our confidence in ourselves, which affects our decisions and ultimately affects the lives of others.

Anita Roddick sums up the *dissatisfied voice*, the nagging, irritating reminder that something can be done about a product or a service you use everyday. It may be a can opener or a way to hang clothes or a bicycle seat that spurs you to create a different product. "My motivation for going into the cosmetics business was irritation: I was annoyed by the fact that you couldn't buy small sizes of everyday cosmetics and angry with myself that I was too intimidated to go back and exchange something if I didn't like it. I also recognized that a lot of the money I was paying for a product was being spent on fancy packaging which I didn't want. So I opened up a small shop to sell a small range of cosmetics made from natural ingredients in five different sizes in the cheapest possible plastic containers."[7]

These two business partners, imagination and intuition, are essential to influence entrepreneurial ideas and decision making. I've given you ideas and articulated them. Now is the time to bring them into your life by working with the following four exercises, tools to increase your skill with these partners to impact your business in a positive way.

EXERCISES

An entrepreneur pilot who owns and operates a successful international charter service once asked me about intuition, how to

---

7. Anita Roddick, *Body and Soul* (New York: Crown, 1991) 19.

understand it better and "how one gets it." While there is no ticket to buy or guaranteed ways I can give imagination or intuition to somebody, I can offer four exercises to help you develop creative thinking through using your imagination and being aware of the intuitive voice.

1. Practice Journaling   "Effective exploration requires effective record keeping,"[8] Buckminster Fuller once commented. This was echoed in my entrepreneurship studies. As part of my MBA course, entrepreneur and advisor Ken Willig required that students keep a journal as a part of the class. We were instructed to think about our business for half an hour a day, and to write about it during that time. This has been one of the greatest pieces of advice given to me, giving me time to reflect about my business, to see what I did well during the day, and where I need to improve. I also use it as a way to look into the future, or simply to mull over some problems, or reflect on a newspaper article which may impact my business positively or negatively.

For example, I had a client company that had two departments that needed to work together for the success of a program. I was brought in when it seemed that the chasm between the two was growing wider and wider. After my first day with them, a day of frustration for everyone, on my way home I opened my journal. I put one department on the left page and one on the right. I wrote down what I remembered of the day, the dialog, the feelings, the body language. As I disengaged from the situation, by getting it down on paper, I began to see patterns, and was able to come up with some strategies for the next day. Without writing it down, it would have been more difficult to detach from the situation, and get away from the value judgments I had assigned myself and others. My creative imagination could then engage to come up with solutions for working with the group the next day.

8. Buckminster Fuller, *Critical Path* (New York: St. Martin's Press, 1981) 128.

Have you ever seen any of the notebooks that great inventors and artists have used to think through problems and use their imaginations, recording their thoughts and feelings? I was inspired by Leonardo da Vinci's *Codex Leicester*, on view at the Seattle Art Museum. Captivated by the creative spirit, I read his thoughts about water and admired drawings of inventions.

Another artist, architect Paolo Soleri, founder of Arcosanti, an intentional community in Arizona, has a collection of notebooks about his architectural visions. These are also incredible drawings and thoughts brought into physical existence.

Notebooks can be orderly, with dividers made for each part of your business life, or they can be without conscious order, just creating things as you go. I usually have a journal with a small ring binding, so it can lay flat when open; one side is for writing, one side for drawing. Other people choose to journal on their computers or talk into a tape recorder to listen to on their drive home.

Sometimes I put in what I call a "Synchronicity Structure." This helps me record my experiences with synchronicity to understand now and at any later time. I use four columns, labeling them "inner thoughts," "outer manifestation," "interpretation," and "themes." On the left side I label the rows as follows:

Date
What time was it?
Who with?
What happened?
How long did the event(s) last?
How I felt at the time.
Feeling that was created. How do I feel now?

Why do I strongly recommend journal writing? First, it is a way to give yourself time to reflect, time to identify and focus on areas of growth for yourself and your business. Second, it is amazing what happens when you give yourself the time to write. The more you honor your creativity by writing or drawing it, the more it comes to visit. The third reason is to inspire you. The journal serves as a milepost of growth and accomplishment and as a way to motivate you even on your most challenging days.

2. Be Aware of Energy   Being aware of your energy may seem simplistic, but when it is overlooked it can spoil your efficiency. A good way to become aware of peak moments during your day is to chart some of your patterns by thinking of peak times of creativity in your life. When do you seem to have the most energy during the day? What are you doing at that time? Are you sitting in meetings when you have the energy to complete the day-to-day detail-oriented tasks? Can you make choices to arrange your schedule because of these needs? This is a specific exercise that will allow you to reflect on high energy times and low times and to make better use of when you think better and when you might need to take a break.

3. Take Time in the Natural World   Being in nature is another way to open creative space. Not only does it get your mind and body into a different place than you normally work in, but you also work with your senses differently, allowing your mind to think in unusual patterns. Inventors and scholars have been known to walk in the woods to think and enhance their awareness of when personal "aha's" appear.

Take a day to enjoy nature—a whole day is the ideal, but even a lunch break can revive you. The natural world, like all relationships, needs time to develop. Although having human companions can be important at times, this is one time you need to be alone with this world. You may choose a park, beach, forest, desert, prairie, or river. A Puget Sound beach is my place of choice. Let me show you how I use these "time out" experiences to make my business and personal life improve.

When I walk the beach, I try to let go of my thoughts and worries as much as I can. I look upon this time as a "vacation from worry." I start off by using my five senses, traditionally recognized as sight, sound, touch, smell, and taste. I spend time with each area slowly, entering into the sense.

Sight is the first area I go to, and is the sense I usually use most. It is when I really look at what I am seeing. What are the colors like? Are they vibrant or muted? How does the light reflect on the water? Is it a sharp white and blue, or a gray? Is it foggy or misty, and how does that affect the light? How is this different from what I usually see?

Next, I go to the sounds I hear. Although I may hear sounds of cars, boats, other people, or airplanes, I can attune to natural sounds. These can be the sounds of the unique wave patterns, subtle at times, or high-wake waves pummeling the shore. I hear birds—seagulls and crows with occasional eagles. I can hear the wind through the crags of the Madrona. How do I hear some sounds and tune out others?

Through the sense of touch, I note how sand feels running through my hands, or under my feet. Is it cold, warm, or hot on a sunny day? Is it misty? raining? How does the wind feel against my skin? Is it soft or biting? How does the drying salt water affect my skin? How tight does my body feel? Am I tense, anxious? Would filling my lungs with air dissipate the tension? How am I holding this unreleased energy?

Smell is the fourth sense, and it is found in the smell of the salty air and water and the plants. When I return from a trip, one of the first things I smell coming back into Seattle is the smell of the Sound. Grasses have their own smells as does seaweed.

Taste, the last of the traditional senses, is found most strongly in the taste of the salt in the wind. If you have brought food or drink with you, find a place where you can sit and enjoy your food. What does a sandwich really taste like? Many of us seem to be unaware of taste when we start to eat. It's as if a switch in our brain tells us to focus on who we are with, what we are talking about, and sometimes, even making a business deal rather than the pleasure of taste. We may pick at a salad, gobble down an entrée, or eat a dessert that later we forgot we had. In this exercise, really pay attention to what your body takes in as food.

A sixth sense lives in the realm of intuition and imagination. Recognize the thoughts that are with you, the inner environment. What do you think of when you can get away? Can you clear your mind or do things keep popping up? Do you go over memories, perhaps something that you need to remember to do when you return to the office? Letting go of your worries and knowing you can work with them later gives you an opening to experience creativity.

You may wonder what application this exercise has on your business or workplace. You may question when you would have time to go to a beach, a lake, or a forest when it would take hours just to get there. What is the point anyway?

The point of this exercise is that during the day we are constantly pulled from our center, our point of balance. When the phone rings incessantly, meetings are numerous, and demands are great from other people, we tend to lose our balance, the fulcrum from which we make our best decisions. We do a disservice to ourselves and ultimately to others when we do not go to center, when we are not aware of how we affect others. It reminds me of Stephen Covey's emotional bank accounts described in *Seven Habits of Highly Effective People*. My focus on these bank accounts is to frame them around keeping the bank accounts balanced in ourselves. We must have time to refuel our entrepreneurial energy.

If you don't have half an hour for lunch during the day, or twenty minutes twice a day, and an hour seems like a luxury, allow yourself to either change, let go of some activities, or combine them. A walk could be combined with the sensory exercise. Another way to make time is to photograph a favorite place and put the photos on your desk. During the day, look at these photos and recall not only in your mind but in your body how it felt to be at these places. At a particularly intense part of my life, I would spend even five minutes in the car in the parking lot (this is not a good idea when you drive!) watching rain drops fall on the windshield and watching the patterns. Put yourself back to center.

The key to this whole exercise is awareness. As we become more aware, we make better decisions about ourselves and the people we work with. Both our intuition and our imagination are clearer. We can play with metaphors in our mind: how does the way the waves act remind me of a dilemma at work? What can I do to calm the storm? Another benefit of this exercise is that it makes us aware of the whole and part of the environment that sustains us. We cannot deny that we impact the environment. We must embrace and care for it if we are to continue to exist here.

I recall talking with an entrepreneur whose company specialized in setting up networks in large corporations. He told me that he took his company to a retreat in the woods to talk about the future of the company. I asked him if he realized how important it was that his company met and interacted with nature. At first, he looked at me as if I was crazy. "What are you talking about?" he snarled. Through metaphors he could understand and as close to his view as I could reach, I told him how the natural world sustains us, is a place to enrich our ideas. By the end of the conversation, although I don't think I convinced him fully to the idea of the necessity of relating to the natural world, I did plant a seed for him to think about how valuable it is to be a part of the network of the whole of life, and in turn, how much we need to care for it, for its own sake, and not merely for what we can take from it.

4. Cultivate Cross-Cultural and Interdisciplinary Awareness

Take time to travel, meeting local people along the way, and cultivate friends from different cultures. Growing up, I had friends who were Japanese, Irish, Pakistani, Native American, African-American, and Chinese. I continue to have friends from different cultures and choose to be around people who have unique disciplines, different spiritual beliefs, and uncommon occupations. I look at how other countries' companies work. For example, reading about Skaltek, a Swedish designer and manufacturer of wire and cable machinery, I discovered that everyone in their business had the same title: Responsible Person. That story influenced the way I taught personal responsibility to people in a government organization.

"Every day, do something that does not compute." Wendell Berry's quote still inspires me and engages my imagination and intuition. I value creative thinking highly in myself and others. Many times I didn't value creativity, or at least not my use of it in the world because it got me into trouble. I sense in many groups that I'm not the only one this has happened to. Many times our creative thinking through imagination and intuition does not make sense and sometimes goes against popular opinion. We do not fit in and sometimes make people around us uncomfortable because we aren't likely to be placed in a box— any box. Now, creativity at all levels in companies is gaining more acceptance because it is being talked about and because of its value in creating and maintaining vibrant and strong companies.

Imagination and intuition are invaluable partners in creative thinking. They can be developed through exercises that embrace reflection, energy, awareness and diversity. Our creative thinking comes from our center. In having exercises that cultivate awareness, we can increase the strength of our decision-making place.

In using a journal to write our thoughts and feelings we build reflection, a valuable learning tool. We think about what we did well during the day, and what we could have done differently. Is there something we need to do tomorrow to change something?

Energy is an important part of our ability to function in this world. When we understand more about our own energy needs and the energy needs of others, we can use that knowledge to be effective in making positive choices.

In seeking diversity, you are looking at the way people think—people who are different from you in many ways. You can gain invaluable perspective from experiences different from your own.

Chapter 6
Pathological Optimism and Setting Goals

A scene opens: You see sand, sun, and the surf of a tropical island. You watch the surf at play until you see a small dot. You follow the dot and realize it is a lone surfer on a board, running for the crest of the waves. You can't believe your eyes, but as you look closer, you see that the waves have names on them, labels of different aspects of thought: doubt, fear, contentment, joy. The surfer waits to catch a wave, a wave called *optimism*.

Entrepreneurs are pathological optimists—it's what gets us through the hard times. Positive thinking is a hallmark of entrepreneurs, because they are continually riding the up-and-down waves of the business cycle. They are very often riding on the edge of the wave and have the faith to keep the board in the water by insisting on their view of a positive future. *Goal setting*, the kin to optimism, means keeping on the board until you reach the shore, shifting your balance as needed, assessing changing situations in your outside environment, and keeping a cool head.

ENTREPRENEURS AND OPTIMISM

Many of the entrepreneurs I interviewed consider themselves "pathological optimists." Judy Wicks, social activist and founder of White Dog Cafe, a restaurant in Philadelphia, Pennsylvania, commented: "This is a characteristic of entrepreneurs, the thought that 'things are going to work out—not to worry, things are going to be OK.'" The attitude is a fearless outlook about everything, that maybe the outcome will be different, but it will still move them forward into the direction of growth. Positive thinking is an intrinsic entrepreneurial tool. If it wasn't in place, entrepreneurs couldn't go through all the uncertainties and disappointments in their businesses, and ultimately, in their lives. You've probably known people who were both optimistic to the extreme and others who are pessimistic to a fault. Do you wonder how people become either one of those ways, or somewhere in the middle?

How Do People Become Optimistic? Some people "inherit" a positive attitude by being nurtured by positive people, and others are positive because they grew up around negative people and rejected the pattern. Still others are "hardwired" positive, and tend to see the world positively no matter what. Many people started their journey of positive thinking with Dale Carnegie's *The Power of Positive Thinking*, or Napoleon Hill and W. Clement Stone's *Success Through a Positive Mental Attitude*.

Companies, corporations, and organizations have objectives of optimism known as *mission statements.* The mission statement declares the highest thinking, the ideal goals of the organization. If you look at Starbuck's mission statement, for example, it begins with the sentence: "Establish Starbucks as the premier purveyor of the finest coffee in the world while maintaining our uncompromising principles as we grow." This tells me that not only do they want to have the best product in the marketplace, but they also value and uphold integrity as well as success. Below the opening sentence of the mission statement are other affirmations of optimism: "Apply the highest standards of excellence . . ."; "Contribute positively . . ."; "Recognize that profitability is essential . . ."; "Provide a great work environ-

ment . . ."; and "Embrace diversity as an essential component . . ."[1] All of these point to optimism.

What about pessimism as a balancing factor here? Doesn't
being a skeptic have a place in companies? Of course. In
Chapter 5 I tell the story of the woman that the sponsor wanted
to kick off of the committee because of her attitude. There is a
difference between pessimistic people and people who are
not "yes people." Yes people are those who will respond positively to every idea because they want to coat your ego, to pat
you on the back, say anything because they think you will like
them better. James Collins and William Lazier's book, *Beyond
Entrepreneurship*, tells us that we need people who disagree
with us, those who say, "Hey! wait a minute, I don't think you
have the whole picture. What if . . ." They serve as a balance or
an alter ego to the optimist or idealist part of the entrepreneur. In
many business situations we have a balance from people different from our ways of thinking because it keeps us from our own
worst mistakes. George Zimmer (The Men's Wearhouse) says
that

> Team building at TMW is based on the premise that because
> nobody is perfect, work teams must be constructed to balance
> strengths and weaknesses of key players . . . This balance
> creates a situation that puts together teams in which the team is
> stronger than the sum of its parts (synergy). TMW is most
> successful when the following elements are successfully
> balanced: individual needs/group; aggression/compassion;
> careful planning/action; interest of all stakeholders (employees,
> owners, stockholders, community). The synchronistic
> experiences I have had have all helped balance these elements
> better and benefit from the more traditional type of synergy.

We have all had experiences when teams were unbalanced.
People of a certain mindset may not take in all of the issues that
need to be addressed in the planning of a product. Teams with

---

1. Howard Schultz, *Pour Your Heart Into It: How Starbucks Built a Company One Cup at a Time* (New York: Hyperion, 1997) 139.

more balance will be more successful, and if they focus on the project and their commonalities, less disturbance will result. Early in my career as a consultant I was working with a group and I was quite anxious going into the second meeting, the first where I would be working directly with my group. The group had previously taken an inventory that segmented their learning styles into four areas. Since the four people in the group had been chosen in advance, I did not know how the team would be balanced. It turned out that all four participants were represented by each of the areas!

With my entrpreneurship students I divide the class into four person teams. The first teams are the "similars." These groups contain people who have similar business ideas. For example, all consultants are together, and all retail store entrepreneurs form a group. The second teams or the "diverse" teams are a combination of entrepreneurs with dissimilar ideas: a team could contain one consultant, one retail store owner, one auto dealer, and one restaurant owner. Both sets of groups are invaluable.

Without optimism, a company goes stale. Ideas are shunned, employee morale hits the bottom, and it has a direct effect on productivity. One of the managers I worked for intentionally created a hostile environment because he believed that anger was a great motivator and made us all work faster. I don't think he realized that this view of motivation was faulty, even after I stated the problems of turnover, increased insurance claims, and absenteeism to him.

Some people simply do not act directly. They do not ask their managers why they have to be led by shame and anger. They will respond by leaving employment if they can, get hurt on the job (not necessarily intentionally), or stay at home. I admit that I did go to another part of the office to isolate myself from working with the anger-motivating manager. It wasn't until I confronted him that I found out that he really did believe that his anger spawned action—but when I asked, "in the short run or long term?" he grew silent. He told me that this method of managing always worked, that people worked faster because they were so furious and worked off their anger. The usual output was half again as much, he said. Why shouldn't he use this technique if it worked?

Fortunately, not all bosses are like this. Mel Bankoff, entrepreneur of Emerald Valley Kitchen of Eugene, Oregon, makers of organic food products (including a fabulous salsa) describes his philosophy of positive goal setting and treating people well:

> Business serves as a means (production and exchange of commodities and for ideas) not an end. It is a process to work with, not to necessarily control with malign intentions either conscious or unconscious. I hold to my convictions of (1) [promoting] organic/sustainable foods, (2) creating a learning organization treating employees financially equitably and supporting their personal growth, and (3) giving part of the success back into the community with donations to needy non-profit service organizations.

The benefits have been outstanding for Mel and both he and his company have benefited by the choices he has made:

> I have seen my co-workers become more empowered and confident in themselves. The growth of organic food availability has skyrocketed since I began my business. I have seen the direct impact of how our business has locally, nationally, and internationally served many people in need. I continue to grow personally and challenge the existing status quo of how and what is possible in the world of business.

In Mel's comments we see three strong aspects of optimistic focus—product analysis, human resource development, and community—as well as our second subject in this chapter, goal setting. He and his company do a wonderful job of creating a delicious product that satisfies the public and satisfies Mel's need to use organic and sustainable foods. In his second goal, Mel meets the needs of his employees, not only through financial compensation but also through personal growth. He is proud of the confidence his employees have and he is a part of their blossoming. There is no need to anger his employees unjustly to motivate them. Mel sees that he has a responsibility to the community in which he does business, and has made meeting that responsibility his third goal. Many businesses honor this responsibility. Some will sponsor people to special events, such as concerts and competitions, or provide college scholarships. Mel assists nonprofit service organizations.

Can you imagine working with Mel? How exciting to be able to see the joys and work through the difficulties of owning a business, and sharing those cycles with employees; he provides the means to increase productivity and confidence, and the ability to take initiative in solving problems.

The clarity and conviction that one can read in Mel's statement is part of what makes him a successful entrepreneur. He is positively focused, envisions the outcome of his goals and the direction he is to take that he sees the benefits, the positive influence toward the people he works with and the community of Eugene. Part of his success comes back to how much of his time and energy is aimed toward the completion of those clear goals.

THE ROLES OF GOALS

Clear goal setting is another area of activity that makes entrepreneurs successful. They may use techniques such as creating and writing ideas down, thinking about their goals in a positive way, creating mission statements, or refining company goals and statements. In the last chapter we talked about journaling and listening to the creative voice. In this chapter, we will take those intentions and work with them further. The following are but three examples of entrepreneurs who see the value of being very clear about the direction they are taking.

Devi Jacobs of Outback, a retail clothing store in Berkeley, California, says that she "operates on synchronicity." Devi makes a list, putting down her needs clearly, not wishing, but knowing strongly that her needs will be met. She says it "has to be clear and definite, and the outcome needs to be wanted and strongly desired."

Marjorie Kelly, of *Business Ethics* magazine echoes the belief that clarity is very important. She "tends to get things that she wants but must be very clear in the right way, and focus on results. Not to focus on what I want X person to do because X person has their own free will. Listening to inner wisdom guidance is crucial." Marjorie's voice is refreshing after listening to plenty of lectures about creating reality when we don't have total control. We must let each other have free will, the ability to act for ourselves, and to accept other people's goals. This is reminiscent of Tom Chappell (Tom's of Maine) who remarked that it's not intuition that is the issue—it is that when our intuitions come together, and they are pointing in different directions, we have to select one direction from there that makes it tricky. Marjorie's inner wisdom, her intuition, is her compass to guide her into the correct decisions that help her move in the direction she wants.

What is important about clear direction is that we commit to a goal, plot the course, and go on to complete the task. In choosing a goal, we are essentially selecting to develop parts of ourselves, our employees, and our companies. Choosing priorities is very important, and to have two or three in your mind at all times can keep you in focus. I have found that in some workplaces it is difficult to keep goals in mind because day-to-day priorities change quickly. The to-do list that day has to change rapidly because of the nature of the business or because of the emergence of external factors.

Another entrepreneur made a poetic comment about clarity: "I stretch when I see the unfamiliar. I like exercises in paradox, when things seem unbalanced, but I find vacations in clarity, and when the path is straight and steady." It is only through goal setting and working on our direction that we can go in a clear direction, which may or may not be a straight path. I am reminded of when I took flying lessons and learned that to stay on course I would have to make a series of corrections in my direction. That is how it is in business. We have to make adjustments to goals to reach our ultimate destination.

Synchronicity can echo the straight and steady. Without so much as a warning, synchronicity can cut a path through the fuzziness and doubt that can creep in, creating a lighthouse beacon in the midst of indecision. It can lift us up on the surf-board again.

EXERCISES

Positive thinking, planning, and intention are mantras that seem to weave a common thread through the stories in this chapter. How can one develop these skills? How can we be as clear and positive about our goals as Mel Bankoff?

1. *What Do I Want? Creating Clarity*   Take a piece of paper, and instead of writing at the top of the page, turn it one-eighth of a turn so you are writing in the corner. Write the answer to the question, "What do I want?" Turn the page a quarter turn to the next corner, and write a different answer to "What do I want?" and then keep turning the page and writing answers, making an inward spiral. If it is difficult to start this exercise, try to do it from a perspective of what others say you want. This will usually get you started. Then be sure to switch to your own perceptions. If you fill the page before you are finished, simply start another page and keep the stream of thoughts going.

This is also an effective method for getting to the core of difficult decisions. As you make your way around the spiral, you will find that the corners provide a way to "peel back the layers", to look at the situation more clearly, and to open up what is underneath the common voice to the deeper thoughts and feelings affecting your judgment.

2. *Personal Mission Statement* A personal mission statement is a declaration of optimism, similar to a corporate mission statement. It clarifies who you are, what your values are, and the direction in which you want your life to be going. Some of these statements are only one sentence while others are short lists of a few items or a paragraph.

Stephen Covey promotes the use of these statements. My mission statement has solved dilemmas in my business life. I have used my mission statement to assist me with choosing projects. For instance, when I think about the opportunities, I hold the written description of the project next to my mission statement and compare the two. Are they congruent? Does this choice make sense to where I want to go in the big picture?

Sometimes people share mission statements with others, and sometimes they are personal, literally. You may choose to share all or parts of yours, or not to share at all. The choice should be left up to the individual. I will share one of my personal mission statements here:

Personal Mission Statement
I want to fly. I want to assist others to fly.

Although I am sometimes confused with the two dimensions of tarmac—my perceptions of my limitations,

I know there is a third dimension where I fly freely—proactively contacting others to understand where they are going; giving each other space; going for the same goals, but allowing each other our variations in getting there;

I strive to keep my emotional wings balanced, my fuel tank of energy filled, and my radio operational to communicate.

I fly cooperatively and respectfully with the birds and others of flight, embrace nature, and have respect for the winds that are out of my control—the clouds that I may face, the lightning that may surprise me, and the thunder that might frighten me—and know that I have the divine knowledge and human experience to solve any dilemma that I might encounter.

Let me always appreciate the glorious sun and stars, and value the joy that is in life. I want to never forget who I am, why I am here, and to know that Spirit lovingly holds me in every thought.

---

3. Ten Commitments   Conrad Hilton, successful entrepreneur of the Hilton Hotel chain, wrote *Be My Guest* in 1957. He insisted that people "Develop your own policy, domestic and foreign. Give it thought. And the effort. Stand on it! Stand for it! Live it!"[2] This quote is found in the section of the book entitled "Assume Your Full Share of Responsibility for the World in Which You Live."

A twist on the mission statement, establishing a personal policy is what I call the ten commitments. This is a list of commitments to yourself, or yourself and others. Take a moment and list the things that are the most important to you, such as your family, excellent health, financial stability, beauty, nature, variety in your work, ability to influence and care for people. Then start to formulate statements that reflect the power of commitment: "I commit to having . . . I commit to improving . . . I commit to helping . . ." You may recognize that all will not be obviously focused on your business. But as entrepreneurs know, the boundary between your work and home life is blurred, and what you write down as your commitments will affect all aspects of your life.

Before I go on to the next exercise, I want to tell you a story of synchronicity. I had been teaching about the ten commitments (a play on the ten commandments) for a couple of years. I picked up a copy of *The Leadership Challenge*, by James Kouzes and Barry Posner, and found that they use the same term as a theme and structure of their book. I highly recommend it.

4. Flash Cards   At the end of each year I choose a letter from the alphabet, one I have not chosen in previous years. I go through the pages of the dictionary, choosing words beginning with that letter that have meaning to me. I may write down a list of 40 words, then narrow the choices to ten words that I can memorize. They have to have deep meaning to me, and have to

2. Conrad Hilton, *Be My Guest* (Englewood Cliffs: Prentice-Hall, 1957) 286.

relate to my focus and intention for that year. For example, one year I chose the letter *E*. I wrote down *electricity, evolution, evaluate, excitement*. Another year I chose the letter *I* and wrote down *intuition, involvement, Incas, Inscape*. All of these words had meaning and reflected the goals of that year. Reading the words every morning "jump starts" my day.

5. It's Always Something If you find yourself resigned to this disparaging comment about a situation, try catching yourself and changing the saying to "it's always something—good." I am not asking you to deny reality here. I am simply asking you to consider a different view, a more optimistic one. Become aware of sayings or clichés you use habitually.

6. Two Obvious Things That Work First, to develop positive thinking skills and goal-setting savvy, spend time and be mentored by people who are optimistic and excellent goal setters. You can watch firsthand how they organize their lives, take what is valuable, and make a system that works for you. You can see how they deflect criticism, put forward their points of view, and how they cope with change.

Second, read biographies and autobiographies for inspiration. Learn what other people did when they were feeling overwhelmed, made mistakes or were discouraged. How did they keep moving toward their goal? Learn how they organized or disorganized themselves. What would they have changed?

Optimism and clear goal setting are important tools in the entrepreneur's tool box. Optimism, a vital light within ourselves, keeps us going through positive and challenging times. Entrepreneurs want to succeed and have the faith to do so by their optimism, and by motivating themselves with the assurance that things will work out. Goal-setting skills give us focus, and help us articulate the future of our organization to the people who are involved in the organization. They keep us going in a true direction, moving forward or changing our strategy if we need to go a different way. After working on our clarity, we are ready to proceed to being more open to possibilities that present themselves.

Sometimes the surfboard slips and we can fall off. But until then, the entrepreneur will ride waves of optimism to the ultimate goal: the shore.

Chapter 7
Being Open to Opportunities

George Zimmer, founder of The Men's Wearhouse, comments that synchronicity is "a normal experience for the individual 'open to the moment' and freed from the constraints of popular opinion. This may be the defining characteristic of the successful entrepreneur." Openness has been touched upon in previous chapters, but we are going to go into more depth here. To be aware of synchronicity, we need to be open to many sources—some uncommon—to solve problems, such as increase client base, invent products, or improve marketing strategies.

In research, writing, and in situations in everyday life I'm constantly amazed by how many times people and places open up to solve the dilemma I have been considering. Like George, I know what it is like to be open to the moment, suspending my judgment about the messenger or the message he/she relayed. I pay attention to what I am listening to and sensing—not just the words, but also the body language of the messenger. I pay attention to how the words are used and, more importantly, the meaning of the words and the essence of the conversation. What in their speech shimmers? What words do I pay attention to? What meanings are between the lines? Can I perhaps bring something out of this conversation to benefit other parts of my life?

I have two stories of synchronistic situations in which I was able to connect with two entrepreneurs that I had wanted to contact because I was open and receptive. I met Paul Wenner, founder of Wholesome and Hearty Foods, Inc., creator of the Gardenburger, through a conversation that occurred at my home. Two years ago I had a housewarming party. There I met a woman by the name of Claire Wehrley. She asked about my dissertation study, which I had completed a few short months earlier. A few minutes into the conversation, she asked, "Do you know Paul Wenner? I used to work with Paul, would you like me to arrange an interview with him?"

She was the public relations manager for Wholesome and Hearty Foods, and with her assistance and the work of The Evans Group, I was able to interview Wenner.

It is important that I uncover my inner psychic state at that time. I was looking for entrepreneurs to interview, to expand my number of stories of synchronistic experiences. I was able to contact an entrepreneur through someone familiar to him instead of hoping to get through to him with phone calls on my own. I was amazed. And it happened at something so casual as a housewarming party! Claire followed through with her offer; Paul did call me a few days later, while he was on a book tour. Our conversation was an excellent one.

In the second situation I had just finished picking up some documents in Seattle and was angry at having to commute a few hours to pick up these papers, ones that could have been faxed. I walked down the hill to the ferry building to sit down and write since I was 45 minutes early for the ferry. Soon after, a man came up to me and asked me what time it was. I said, "6:30." He asked when the next boat was, and I told him it left at seven.

He left, only to return about 10 minutes later. "Do you mind if I sit next to you?" I scanned the room and no one else was there. I said yes, of course, thinking "why does he want to sit next to me? Can't he see I am writing and there are plenty of other seats!"

But, I put my paper down and talked to him for quite a while, and he asked what I was writing. When I told him about my study and the entrepreneurs already involved, he pointed to his shoes. "Do you have the woman who founded this shoe company in your study?" I read the company name imbedded in the sole of the shoe: Deja Shoe. "Would you like to speak to Julie Lewis, the founder?" I had heard of her innovative product and company for years and had wondered how I could arrange an interview with her, so accepted his offer eagerly. He said, "I'm meeting with her tomorrow at ten. I'll give her your card and let her know about your study." Steve Sunde did just that.

In both cases I was very surprised and speechless! I wanted so much to meet the entrepreneurs they knew, but I also knew that sometimes I had to call entrepreneurs multiple times just to find a few minutes in their schedules to talk. It was amazing how easy it was just to be present, to be vulnerable, to look for the opportunity and accept the gift that people offered to me. I was also amazed at how I could feel so irritated at something, yet have the interruption bear fruit. If you have seen the movie *Field of Dreams*, you might remember when Ray gets very angry at his daughter for interrupting him while he and Annie are going through the financial books for the farm. Annie is disclosing that the farm is in jeopardy because of the baseball field. They both are trying to figure out some options. The daughter is incessant in her interruption. "Dad! Dad!" Ray finally asks what she wants, and she says, "there's a man in your baseball field." It is this breaking down to the moment, in spite of despair and being upset, that got Ray and me through our situations.

Louise Hay, author of *You Can Heal Your Life*, says that the people you are searching for can be contacted through the people you already know. The premise of the movie *Six Degrees of Separation* is that everyone we want to know is within six people from us, and the first person to contact is someone we already know. Paramahansa Yogananda, author of *Autobiography of a Yogi*, referred to the importance of opportunities: "Your success in life does not altogether depend on ability and training; it also depends on your determination to grasp opportunities that are presented to you."[1]

You may refute me here, and say that for every person who wants to help you (or even more, depending on your optimistic/pessimistic scale) there are just as many who do not want to help, who will put obstacles in your path. I will not deny that there are people who do that intentionally as well as unintentionally. However, being the optimist that I am, I know through my study that many people kept on their path, being wiser for the obstacles and choosing allies more carefully. Julie Lewis mentioned that sometimes synchronistic experience takes us down a path we may not enjoy but that we gain experience, and should follow it anyway. Again, we cannot be in control of everything. Synchronicity works in a way that baffles us, that works out of our control, and ignores our traditional beliefs of causality.

Synchronicity can be noticed in two different ways. The first is when an outer event occurs that can mirror the inner thought, and the second is when the outer event happens first, wakening and surprising the inner desires and hopes we hold. Being open to possibilities and opportunities and awareness of the clues and cues in one's life is so important. What goes into our thoughts through our own filters establishes our knowledge and beliefs, and influences our decision making and what we see or choose to see in our life. So, we're reflected in a mirror of inner process/outer event. The inner process enables the question: What can I do with this opportunity? The outer event is the actual possibility in the physical world.

There are four elements that I have identified that describe areas of being "open to the moment," as George Zimmer referred to it. These areas are awareness, trust, openness to personal change, and removal of obstacles.

---

1. "Self-realization Fellowship," *Inner Reflections Calendar* (Los Angeles: Self-realization Fellowship, 1997) unnumbered.

AWARENESS

This story is from Margery Miller, an entrepreneur in Dallas, Texas. In addition to owning a firm selling commercial food service equipment, she also created People in Business, a company dedicated to developing people in small and medium sized businesses to reach their full potential.

Margery says, "I realized there were many people who needed help to do the things I had considered standard operating procedure in my own business. Most companies have very little experience or know-how in people development. I would find myself calling on a dealer to sell them equipment and ended up giving them advice on what to do with their staff. This happened so many times that I realized I was probably better at working with people than selling equipment. I remember one of my first clients was my doctor's office. I just happened to mention that I was doing work for a few people and she immediately hired me. So in a way, my business was created out of synchronicity. I seemed to be at the right place at the right time and just by talking about my passion would create business for myself. At the same time, my own company continued to grow in a way that allowed me plenty of freedom to do the other things that were important to me."

Margery is an ace of awareness. She picked up on clues that dealers she was selling equipment to needed more than a freezer or mixer. She was able to convey her knowledge and wisdom on human resources issues. I am amazed that she started talking about her business at the doctor's office. I'm not surprised that she did that, but that her doctor was one of her first clients! How many opportunities do you find in the course of a day that you might be missing?

Dave Potter, founder of the high-tech company Concurrent Sciences, and of the consulting firm Discovery–Dialogue–Direction Inc., told me that awareness is key, that when you become aware of opportunities they seem to appear all over the place. For example, if you buy a Jeep, you will suddenly notice how many other Jeeps there are on the road. Greg Steltenpohl (of Odwalla) refers to this awareness when he remarks that he "constantly watches for omens." He looks for those times when it feels right to tell people what he does and to ask if they need his help. They are openings, these envelopes of time that Thomas Makray called opening of a window, and what Carlos Castenada called the square centimeter of chance.

At times we are timid. We are afraid of being rejected, afraid of setting ourselves up for disappointment, harm, or regret. It may be something we experienced early on, but it harms us when we cannot take risks when we feel that inner voice coaxing us to open up, to give more information about ourselves, to be like Joe Jaworski at the airport meeting his wife-to-be, Mavis.

A trusting response toward our inner selves eventually expresses itself in the external world. Can we trust ourselves to say the right words, to be the people who attract synchronistic events? Can we trust others?

TRUST

I feel that the more you develop awareness and trust, the more open you are to developing synchronicity. Kathy Gardarian of Qualis International explained her awareness and timing this way:

> Many times you will notice that synchronicity will occur in the appropriate timing. The second you act like everything is synchronicity, the more obvious it will become. Trust. It is a knowingness. You simply take it for granted that everything you are perceiving is synchronicity. No accidents! And the way you relate to it is the way you need to. Know that it will always manifest in whatever way it needs to.

Kathy is saying that synchronicity will become obvious once you've acknowledged that you desire it and made the commitment to let this awareness come into your life, trusting that it will manifest in the way it needs to, out of your control and my control.

Contractor Jack Rafn also believes that synchronicity will manifest the way it needs to. He gives two examples of the way it has worked for him, once when things worked out well when he didn't get the project bid, and once when things worked out when a bid was successful. He says that synchronicity "occurred in the projects we didn't get. Projects I really wanted, that would advance our position in the marketplace. Invariably, the successful contractor suffered losses on the project that would have wiped out our company. The other side is getting a phone call that allowed us to enter a market we had never considered and allowed us a dominant position with higher margins than our usual markets."

Both Kathy and Jack trust themselves and trust that they will make the right decisions for their company based on their knowledge and awareness of subtle clues that they might be able to pick up on.

OPENNESS TO PERSONAL CHANGE

Some entrepreneurs, and I include myself, blur the boundaries between personal and business life. Our business threads into our personal lives, and our personal lives weave into our business. I see my business self in every aspect of what I do. In this section, I am going to include two stories that focus on change; one from a business perspective and the other from a personal viewpoint.

But first, one of the points I want to make is that everyone, in business or not, needs to have this aspect of personal change. Neither awareness nor trust is enough by itself. To grow is to be open to personal change, not only cognitive of it, but to be aware of it as something meaningful. In every group or team that I have worked with, it is much easier to work with people who are open to personal change, not just organizational change. It's thrilling to me when people who work together on a project grow and blossom as a result of it, whether they learn how to interact more successfully and graciously in groups; sell their ideas to a larger group; or gather support and defend their project, moving it into areas that far surpass where they started or their expected outcome. The next story will help illustrate how personal change can play a part in building a business.

Mark Juarez is the founder of Tender Loving Things, maker of the Happy Massager®, a four-legged massage tool that saves the wrists of massage therapists from injury. He relates:

> I was touring Europe on my bicycle. I injured my knee to the point that I could no longer ride my bike. The prognosis was not good. Surgery was called for with only a 50 percent chance of success. I decided to go to Berlin to visit a friend and it was there that synchronicity started playing a noticeable role in my life.
>
> While in Berlin, I was sitting in a tiny cafe with my friend. He got involved in a heated discussion with another person, and not being interested in the subject at hand, I began to talk to a woman who sat at the next table. This woman had just completed a course in massage and was beginning to fulfill her practical training requirements. She offered to massage my knee for free and it was then that I was first introduced to what I soon realized was my calling. I went beyond simply receiving massage, and began to take classes at a massage institute. I could soon see and feel the benefit massage had in my life, and in the lives of people I worked on.

Mark was open to change. He was up against a major decision, whether or not to have surgery with only 50/50 odds of success, and all of us want better odds than that. He was open enough to turn to another person, start talking, and to receive a knee massage from a stranger! Again, awareness and trust were there as components, but the real jump was to be open to receiving new information. New information about massage, something he had not experienced before, and then to have the idea. "Hey, wait a minute . . . I really like the benefits that massage has given me." What is crucial here is his decision to become a massage therapist, to not only receive but to give massage. This was not only for a personal healing, but the passion for massage and wanting to continue it for others that built his company.

The following personal story comes from a friend, a teacher who had a meaningful experience that introduced her to synchronistic experiences. She went to a wellness conference in order to get more ideas for her curriculum, to update her classes. Little did she suspect that she would get more information than she hoped for.

> I was going to a wellness conference. It was a three-day seminar in a distant city, during the summer, and included a mix of several classes to do with fitness, diet, and health. I attended a class that included a guided meditation, something I had not done before. Part of the meditation was being guided to a place where a being of some sort would talk with me. It turned out to be a bluebird. The bird was very unexpected as I really thought a wise man or woman would come out from behind the trees. I imagined this bird, and it was telling me about the next steps I could take with my life. The meditation ended shortly after my imagined consultation with the bird. I didn't think much more about it, and the conference ended the next day.
>
> I drove home, picked up the mail, and walked up the stairs into the apartment. I opened the door, and put the stack of mail down on my way to opening the patio sliding glass door. It was then that I saw it. A feather. A bluebird feather was on the floor of the patio! I have never before or since seen a bluebird feather there. It was meaningful to me because the whole guided meditation process was new to me and because of my surprise at seeing a bluebird feather on the patio. It had never happened before! It was life-changing for me.

Both people in the stories were changed as a result of these synchronistic experiences. One went into a cafe, perhaps just to have a chat with a friend. The other was going to a conference to get information to update lectures. Little did they know that by being open, situations would change their lives, give direction, and assist with their personal healing.

REMOVAL OF OBSTACLES

The fourth element of synchronicity is a feeling of obstacles being removed. Judy Wicks (of White Dog Cafe) remarks, "Synchronicity feels less like a miracle, and more like obstacles being removed. Hundreds of little things come together. A 'something is helping me' sense to a certain extent. I wouldn't call it lucky."

Judy is talking about some of the obstacles that have been removed during the development of her restaurant. Some were financial, some were having the right people walk through the door to help her develop the business. Mel Bankoff talks about the need for him "to step aside, to allow the information to come forth." The obstacles can be preconceived notions or plans that have been put into place. Kathy Gardarian (of Qualis International) explains how she overcame the barrier of a former employer:

> I left a large firm to start my own company, and that firm put up a lot of resistance out in the marketplace to my using the same products and manufacturers. Every time I seemed to come up against another "barrier," the right person, thing, or circumstance would "show up" in my life! You always attract the ideas you believe you are willing to act upon, in the manner you are willing to act upon them. I am always fascinated by how well orchestrated everything is that you find yourself participating in—on an unconscious level. Synchronistic events always show me how much control we really have in our lives.

I have found that to be so in my life. In Chapter 6 where I talk about my calls with Paul Wenner and Julie Lewis through the help of Claire Wehrley and Steve Sunde, I consider both Claire and Steve as removers of obstacles for me.

One day I interviewed a middle manager, Kevin, who was in charge of a conversion project, taking a manual process and automating it. He told me what a positive and competent boss said to him when Kevin was in an entry-level position. The boss said to him the first day, "Your job is to do your best. Mine is to remove obstacles that keep you from doing your best." What a refreshing role model.

EXERCISES

1. The Delphic Priestesses Instructed: Know Yourself How well do you know things about yourself that help you in your everyday life? What is the best way you learn? By sitting in lectures, with the ability to gather information through hearing and occasionally with visualiza-tion? Or do you learn best from a lot of visuals, punctuated by someone explaining the concepts? Or do you learn best by doing? It's also important to know your motivation style. Do you work best under the pressure of a deadline? Are you a person who needs to have things in order before you can begin? Do you need to plot your progress, take a step at a time?

It's important to know how you learn. Because we have so much information coming at us quickly, and we need the ability to learn at high speeds to be able to be competent at our jobs, we need to find a format that works for us. I need to have visuals, and learn best by doing. Some people I know can listen to a lecture and gain information without needing to take notes. Others cannot sit through lectures successfully, and start to squirm after a few minutes.

We can see these styles of learning in managers. Some must look at things to make sure that everything is in place. A floor manager in manufacturing may get information by listening to people who come into his or her office. A library manager may manage by walking around, matching the movement, or kines-thetic, with the visual.

I also know people have emotional styles, everything from aggressive and reactionary to inward to passive-aggressive. How do you respond when you do not get a raise? When your coworker gets a promotion that you thought you deserved?

2. Awareness Exercise Enliven all your senses. Write what you are sensing: auditorially—hearing crunching metal, sirens, bells; visually—seeing numbers or symbols, feathers, bus billboard messages; through smell (olfactorily)—fragrances and odors are one of our strongest memory sensor pathways; tactilely—wind on your face, rain, snow; through taste— bitterness, sweetness, sourness.

How does this affect you in your workplace? Being aware of your surroundings makes it easier to pick up on the clues that make you aware of opportunistic openings. Remember what Margery Miller did at her doctor's office. A subtle awareness proved itself and she gained a new client.

We've walked together through the territory of openness, learning how we can continue to be open to the moment when we feel shut down. Tools we discussed in this chapter include awareness, trust, openness to personal change, and the removal of obstacles. Here are some thoughts to reflect upon regarding the four elements of being open to opportunities:

> Awareness: In everyday interaction, are you aware of what clients say to you? Do you know of how you affect other people?
>
> Trust: Do you trust yourself? Whom do you trust? Is it difficult for you to trust other people?
>
> Openness to personal change: Do you let yourself change as you need to, without blocking or ignoring what positive things could happen to you?
>
> Removal of obstacles: Are you aware of people who intentionally go out of their way to remove obstacles? Are you grateful for the opportunities that life gives you?

Debashis Chatterjee commented in *Leading Consciously: A Pilgrimage Toward Self Mastery*:

> Synchronicity in our internal dialogue and external communication means that we are in touch with our spontaneity. The

energy of thoughts and the energy of speech come together in this synchronicity. Speech becomes free flowing like the course of a river from which all obstacles have been removed. Such a speech carries with it the power of dynamism. Communication that originates from the core of the Self has an irresistible natural power like that of heat and light.[2]

2. Debashis Chatterjee, *Leading Consciously: A Pilgrimage Toward Self-Mastery* (Boston: Butterworth-Heinemann, 1998) 121.

Chapter 8
Balancing Goals and Opportunities with Competence

"Tom's of Maine has an obligation to stay in business; it is our moral responsibility to our shareholders and employees to stay alive. . . . If our strategy to manage for profit and the common good fails . . . then we have no alternative but to sell our equity to the competitor whom we believe can best offer job security while maintaining our values and while growing our brand."[1] That is the voice of Tom Chappell. He knows that he must balance his company's vision with making a profit. He must provide a way to make the company grow and maintain responsibility toward shareholders who invest in his vision and the employees who carry it out. For a company to profit and grow, both must be cared for properly.

What is competence? Is it something we can determine by meeting X, Y, and Z criteria? Or do we understand it better when it is missing? Or when we feel that people are totally incompetent, unable to answer the simplest questions, often leaving us to wonder why they are in the positions they are in or how they got

1. Tom Chappell, *The Soul of Business* (New York: Bantam, 1993) 193.

their jobs in the first place. Competence, like synchronicity, can be hard to pin down. We can only begin to measure it in certain ways, knowing that there are still important aspects of people that cannot be measured in a test, an assessment, or a review.

Before I wrote this chapter I thought competence was one of those qualities that was strictly measurable. Can I read and understand a procedures manual? Can I write a report? Can I make this product have higher quality standards? The more I reflected on it, the more I saw competence as an umbrella over two sides of a balance sheet—one side had the "hard" skills I just described. The other side had skills that had to do with intuition, recognizing opportunities, providing high customer service. Competence is the mastery and integration of all these skills.

I would like to tell a story about Henry Ford. At one time he was involved in a lawsuit, one where the prosecutor wanted to prove Ford ignorant. The attorney asked Ford when events in history had occurred, "When did the battle of thus and so occur?" To which Ford replied, "I don't know." Who signed this document? "I don't know." Finally Ford got so fed up that he said, "If I should really want to answer the foolish question you have just asked . . . let me remind you that I have a row of electric push buttons on my desk and by pushing the right button, I can summon to my aid men who can answer any question I desire to ask concerning the business to which I am devoting most of my efforts. Now . . . why should I clutter my mind with general knowledge . . . when I have men around me who can supply any knowledge I require?"[2]

A Seattle entrepreneur I spoke with told me she has to keep a small file of quick information that is important to the running of her business, and that it is impossible to keep everything in her mind at once. "I find it difficult to exist without my files and computer and day planner. I have too many clients, notes, and ideas to remember everything off the top of my head."

2. Napoleon Hill, *Think and Grow Rich* (New York: Fawcett Crest, 1937) 76–77.

This points to an interesting thing about entrepreneurs. They are not only involved in one facet of their company, they are involved in all of the areas of the business. They have to be the ultimate decision makers, being able to balance many areas with competence in order to have outcomes that are positive, or be able to correct situations to the best of their ability. This sometimes makes them seem aloof or detached, overly obsessed and not able to be present at times. Some small business owners I work with seem overwhelmed at times with the high number of things they have to do. They wonder sometimes if they are seen as incompetent, or why they themselves feel incompetent.

Still others wonder about procrastination, and how that makes them feel incompetent. What I recognize in the entrepreneurs I work with is that it isn't procrastination that gets in the way, but overloading with tasks, meetings, and obligations. The antidote is not to think of yourself as incompetent, but to develop the ability to establish and change priorities and give some of your work to others. Delegation is one of the most important abilities that entrepreneurs must possess to stay in business. There is simply no way that one person can do it all.

Three entrepreneurs talk about the balance between your company vision and the feedback, or payback as in this case.

In *The Inside Scoop*, Ben & Jerry's Homemade founder Ben Cohen described a board meeting where they were discussing Ben's vision and its impact on company profits. "Everyone agreed that we needed to make money, not just to survive, but also to create a model that other businesses might follow."[3] Ben has made a balance of hard and soft competence skills through compensation quota policies and employee, community, and vendor benefits. The money the company will make (and has made) is an example of how this balance can happen.

A historical view of corporate philanthropy comes from a story from Polaroid. Henry Morgan, a board member for Ben & Jerry's, "related his experience at Polaroid with its founder,

---

3. Fred "Chico" Lager, *Ben & Jerry's: The Inside Scoop* (New York: Crown, 1994) 182–183.

Edwin Land, who had been one of the first business leaders to boycott South Africa in a protest of its policy of apartheid."[4] Morgan says, "Land would have considered the policy a flop if no one had followed him." The point being that when a business leader takes a big step, there are also big risks.

What happens when an entrepreneur, who has explained passionately her view of social change, comes across an employee who has a different point of view from the vision conveyed to everyone including employees, consumers, and stockholders?

Anita Roddick, owner of The Body Shop, explains how an employee interpreted company goals without balance: "Every now and then we had someone who got it all about face and thought her primary job was to love the world rather than to trade . . . [She] told me how worried she was by a memo that had gone round the shops talking about selling. "Surely we're not here to *sell*?"[5]

An entrepreneur must balance business principles with future trends and common sense. As an entrepreneur you must know the everyday world of accounting, pay taxes on time, motivate employees, and all the while, serve your customers. You need to read future trends, understand the impact of regulation, know the needs of the environment, and take action in the changing face of global interaction. You must have excellent decision-making skills, the ability to stand up for what you believe, and be able to keep going in spite of what is or is not in your control. If any of those facets are not successfully cared for with competence, you cease to be in business.

Enter an entrepreneur's day: meetings all day long, phone, fax, and e-mail messages piling up. At the end of the day, after managing a delivery that was incorrect and hiring two new employees in between the meetings, a stack of phone messages greet you as you sit down at your desk. You go through the

4. Ibid.
5. Anita Roddick, *Body and Soul* (New York: Crown, 1991) 154.

notes: someone inviting you to speak at a service organization meeting next week, a student wants to interview you, and a charity asks for a donation. Under that are letters, then training catalogues, stationery company information, and the advertisements for long-distance phone options. No wonder we feel hopeless about our competence some days.

Mel Bankoff (of Emerald Valley Kitchens) comments about the balance he finds in his business: "Being both open to the world of possibility and the assertion of willfulness with clear intention to bring form into manifestation. The creation and development of my business has been very untraditional both in product development, political stance, and sales connections. The interesting balance to this intuitive preponderance is that I am a 'cautious Capricorn' with a natural proclivity to numbers, and a tenacious worker."

Whether "cautious Capricorn" or a "take-charge Leo," used as a belief in astrology or as a metaphor, entrepreneurs must integrate balancing techniques with their visionary drive.

THE BALANCE STATEMENT

Gary Hirshberg of Stonyfield Farms described "listening to cues as another form of the balance statement." When creating his company, he explains how he had to use his gut sense and his ability to reconcile inner and outer signals and feelings. Perhaps what Gary alludes to is a different way of looking at a balance sheet. Traditionally, a balance sheet shows the balance of assets and liabilities, what you have available in cash, inventory, equipment, and so forth, compared to bills you have to pay. A balance sheet gives you information about the equilibrium of an organization. What I interpret Gary saying is that he notices a "signals" balance sheet.

I see a synchronicity event as a "consciousness feasibility plan." A traditional feasibility plan is somewhat like a business plan, but more concise, much shorter in length. It gives the reader, the entrepreneur and interested parties, an idea of how feasible, or realistic, this proposed business will be. The feasibility plan answers the questions: Will this venture make money? Does it make sense for my life and what I want to do? Do I have the right people to help me? Synchronicity acts like a consciousness feasibility plan as it verifies the inner states that we hold. Are we ready to go forward with this plan? Are things in the outer physical world lining up in place, inviting us to go forward?

Synchronicity acts as a catalyst to get us going. Everyone in relationships is motivated by things that are familiar. It can manifest itself in the forms of word-of-mouth advertising or feeling familiar surroundings when we travel. When synchronicity happens, a little trigger of familiarity goes off inside us, a nudge to let us know it's okay to keep going.

Competency can be like that.

EXERCISES

Create a plan, three to five pages long, integrating the following:

1. Make a chronological chart of your successes and reflect on the years when they happened and their turning points. Think about the critical decisions in your life. Would you change any of these if you could? What have been your most valuable contributions? Times of success? Look back at your life in increments: one year, five years, ten years.

2. Take the same chart and share with people who can give you honest feedback. How did your decisions affect their lives? What is *their* take on *your* success? Are there times you are critical of yourself for making a crummy mistake, but another person says that was not as big an issue as you made it? Are there instances of events that you thought were successful but that affected people other than you thought?

3. Along the same lines, develop and cherish business relationships with mentors and communities of peers. This is

similar to an exercise of gathering mentors who can show you their styles of decision making. These people can push you to higher heights, help you solve problems, keep you aware of developments in the workplace, and (if you are lucky) let you know when you are working against yourself. They can help develop your competence.

4. Take vacations and times of renewal. Leaders must take time out to be competent, to listen, to not burn out. Jamie Sams wisely said, "Negativity is drawn to you when you refuse to give yourself the time and space needed to assume a new viewpoint."[5] Yet sometimes we find making time for ourselves very difficult to do on a consistent basis.

5. Develop lifelong learning skills, curiosity, and a passion for learning. Our occupations are changing as much as the world is and our K-12 and college education is not enough. We constantly have to keep up on new procedures, ways of doing business, and the influx of regulations.

5. Jamie Sams and David Carson, *Medicine Cards* (Santa Fe: Bear & Company, 1998) 191.

Chapter 9
Taming Risk, Taking Action

One of my sisters gave me the best advice for getting things done. She sent a letter shortly after I started my freshman year of college. The following paragraph was included at the bottom of the letter:

> . . . when you are given an assignment in a class, start on it the same day. You don't have to complete it, just spend time with it. Jot down some ideas, people to contact about the subject, key words for a library search, outline of how you would structure your paper. The purpose of this is to get you started and create some motion and motivation to get the assignment complete. Love, your Sis.

That letter has been one of the most important for my success, not only in school, but in business and personal life. It was a way to move things from the abstract to the physical world. As an entrepreneur, I cannot let my goals and dreams exist just in my imagination. I feel an urgency to get things out of my thoughts and into a physically expressed form. This can be in the form of taking notes, doing research, talking with people, writing down and pursuing goals, or getting projects completed. I look to having synchronicity help me know when "the right place at the right time" window is open, that my research and incubation time is now ready to come together. I hedge my risk factors by being able to go when I see that crossroad, that junction.

Another advisor repeated my sister's advice, adding that every idea deserves to have five minutes of your time when the idea pops into your mind. When you end a phone conversation, or after a meeting, give yourself time with that idea and write it down. If you think this is not worth the time, think how many times you have thought of something, didn't act on it, and later saw it on the market. Do you remember the regret you felt or perhaps still feel? Those first five minutes after an idea is given to you are gold. This is a part of you, learning to take action with your ideas. Sometimes it feels very risky to take these actions, such as making an initial "cold" phone call, or time consuming in that you have to rearrange your priorities in order to start some research.

I remember a particular time when the "I could have done that" feeling seized me. It was a number of years after my original idea, but the market opened wide when it hit. I was doing research for a paper in the downtown Portland, Oregon library and I took a break to look at other books a couple of rows away. I noticed there was only one book about angels, the one authored by Billy Graham. I thought to myself . . . Hmmm . . . only one book about angels. I could write a book about angels! Well, needless to say, I didn't write one then, and look what has happened with angels in the last five to ten years—the profusion of books, cards, T-shirts, drinking mugs, and more. I would have been ahead of my time!

Along with taming risk, calming your fears, and being able to have both the know-how and faith (discussed in the previous chapter), is being able to act. Something I noticed with not only the entrepreneurs who were part of my study but others I know, is taking the five minutes to think about and write down your idea, then taking advantage of what is known as the "24 hour-window." This 24-hour period of time after you get an idea is a time of incubation, a time to get very clear about what you want to happen, and to be aware of signals to move forward or to hold steady.

Jackie Sa's story about verification in Chapter 3 related how she found the location of her new business by describing her needs clearly: "I want my business to be located in Mill Valley, California." This is an example of what I call the 24-hour principle. Brian Tracy, in his cassette tape series, "The Psychology of Achievement," suggests that whenever a creative idea comes into mind, you should start working on it within 24 hours. Three of the entrepreneurs I interviewed had situations that mirrored his statement. They clearly stated what they wanted, went to work on the idea or situation within 24 hours, and within a time period of three days to a week manifested what they wanted exactly or so closely to the original idea that it surpassed the probability of chance.

Three entrepreneurs I interviewed, other than Jackie Sa, live and work in three unique geographical areas of the United States with three diverse industries: food products, publishing, and building contracting.

Gary Hirshberg told me that on the morning I called him for his interview, he had had three problems in seemingly unrelated issues, but when all three were joined together they created a solution. This brings the 24-hour principle into practice. At the end of this chapter is an exercise to become aware of what happens in the first 24 hours after you have had an idea. This exercise may help you determine how various seemingly unrelated themes weave together to form an answer or a direction you may wish to take.

John Renesch, creator of business anthologies of over 300 visionary authors, noticed the three-day rule. On one of the projects he hoped to launch, he received a call offering a complete match to what he needed to launch within three days of his decision to pursue the project. And there was no logical way that the person calling could have known he was interested in that particular project.

Jack Rafn related a story of how he had tried to convince an employer for ten years to take him on as a partner. One day the employer implicitly said that it was no longer an option. Jack went home to bed. His wife came in and asked if he would pray about this with her. One hour later, an acquaintance from his son's activity group called and asked for some advice. Within a week he was starting to build his own business.

What about the voice of the skeptic here? Some may say that things could take 36 hours or 72 $\frac{1}{2}$ hours so how can you say that 24 hours makes a difference? I'm saying that 24 hours seems to be the norm with the entrepreneurs I spoke with. I think some of this has to do with energy, something we discussed in Chapter 5. Notice when you first get an idea, how much energy you have in your body; you're excited about what this idea can mean, how you can carry this idea forward, get other people involved. Usually, when inspiration strikes, it strikes deep. It's akin to an incessant telephone ring, the caller wondering when you will pick up and act upon this important message, write it down and make it real.

But how do we know if the call is for us? How can we deal with the risks, the "what if's" that could happen? Sometimes it's hard to even think about risk when we have lost money or relationships because of acting on less than the total picture. But for a moment, think of the times you did take a risk and felt the thrill of victory of jumping off the high dive at a swimming pool, asking for a date, or climbing a mountain. How did it feel? Can you have this feeling again when you make decisions and they turn out well, or even when you make the best out of a bad situation and it turns out much better than expected.

There are times when we can't tell whether it's the fear of the situation that holds us back or if we really are not meant to follow this route. When we develop our intuition and know ourselves and our motives more clearly, we will often know the difference.

EXERCISES

You may ask, "How can I react to situations, have time to spend with ideas when I have so many things going on right now? I am so far behind with projects that I planned two years ago! I can't even keep up with my work projects!" The first exercise will help you to take action against the feeling of despair and being overwhelmed.

1. Clean House
    Like cleaning a room in your house, it is necessary to clean your mind of unwanted or not useful memories. It's not healthy to continue to rerun your bad memories like someone who is memorizing dates for a history class. If you clean out the clutter you will have more time and energy to take action on your thoughts—immediately! It is especially noteworthy to look at how much time you spend in emotional energy over something that may actually take five or ten minutes to do.

2. Complete Your Incompletes
    When you clean out a room, or clear your mind, you are creating room for something more, something different, to take its place. It is a good idea to actually write down what you haven't completed that you really want to do. That way you'll have time to take advantage of your synchronistic experiences.
    Write down and reflect on the following:
    Projects to complete
    Promises I've made
    Example: Things I want to do but haven't done
    1. Fix closet hinge
    2. Take my spouse to a bed and breakfast
    3. Finish novel
    4. Write letters
    5. Take a day off to hike
    6. Go to a movie

Perhaps you want to make a second list concerning your employees. Have you promised to look into a new health care plan? New furniture? Improved lighting?

You may decide to let go of the projects, renegotiate, or let others complete them. Perhaps, for instance, you decide to call a repair person to fix the hinge. It gets done and you are freed for other things.

3. Pay Attention to the Next 24 Hours
From the moment you read this, be aware of what happens to you in the next 24 hours. Think of and write ideas as they come to you. Attend to intuitive voices inside of yourself. Literally stop what you are doing, or if you are doing something you cannot stop at the moment, keep a reservoir in your mind, with a word to anchor your thoughts.

Take a few minutes during the day to let the idea come to fruition. Spend five positive minutes with it, turning it around in your mind. Draw it on a piece of paper. Outline ideas, people to contact to gather more information. How are you a participant to this idea, how can you to move it forward into life? Take the whole five minutes.

That night, take five minutes more. If you haven't already outlined steps and the preferred action to each one of them, do it now. Can you imagine the future you have assigned to each one of the steps? What does success look like?

Make a short plan to put the first steps into action within the first 24 hours. Some calls can be made that night, while other conferences or steps can be made in the morning.

Remember the entrepreneurs that used urgency for their way of getting things done? Within 24 hours kernels of ideas will start popping!

Write to me! I would like to know the stories and experiences that occurred within the first 24 hours, and all synchronistic experiences. I can be reached at P.O. Box 2133, Vashon Island, WA 98070 USA or via e-mail at satori@wolfenet.com.

Take a look at what you wanted to do or wish you could have done, any regrets, situations, and things you really wanted to do differently at various times of your life, and let them go. Truly let them go. You may need to write them on a piece of paper and literally burn that paper or tear it up. If this is difficult for you, remember that the payoff of the 24-hour window depends on this exercise, being able to wipe away things that act against our energy, freeing us to take advantage of fresh ideas, and participate in synchronicities that will occur.

Entrepreneurs can't rest on their laurels; they must take action and keep developing their ideas to bring them into fruition. Jung noted, "That is what we usually neglect to do. We allow the images to rise in us, and maybe we wonder about them, but that is all. We do not take the trouble to understand them let alone draw ethical conclusions from them. . . . It is equally a grave mistake to think that it is enough to gain some understanding of the images and that knowledge can here make a halt. Insight into them must be converted into an ethical obligation (action)."[1]

1. Carl Gustav Jung, *Memories, Dreams, Reflections* (New York: Vintage, 1961) 192–193.

Chapter 10
We Belong to the Web of Life: Interconnectivity

"Man did not weave the web of life . . . Whatever he does to the web, he does to himself."[1]

Ted Perry Inspired by Chief Seattle

Nothing happens by accident. Everything that appears to us can be interpreted in different ways. We meet people who may be friends who will help us, mentors who guide us, or people who, because of jealousy or hurt, will block our progress. At times we have probably done or will do the same to other people. Synchronicity happens in order to awaken us to the possibilities, and some would say the probability, of being connected. It reminds us that there are connections that surpass what we think is possible. Our challenge is to act upon the opportunities synchronicity offers, and do so with integrity.

1. Ted Perry, *How Can One Sell the Air?: Chief Seattle's Vision*, edited by Eli Gifford and Michael Cook (Summertown, NJ: The Book Publishing Company, 1992) 47.

Margery Miller commented: "I believe synchronistic experiences are normal occurrences. I truly believe that all life operates in divine order, and nothing that happens is an accident. That doesn't mean that we are subject to predetermined fate, it merely means we are consistently and continually given opportunities to respond to what the universe expresses forth—and it is up to us to respond in any way we see fit. I feel this applies in all aspects of life, business not being an exception."

What is *divine order*? What is *the universe*? Are these terms used to put smoke in front of my eyes? If you have trouble with these words, you can substitute other words that do make sense to you. Even if you don't believe there is a divine order, you probably have had days that you were able to travel through all green lights all the way to work, a day when every customer you called was genuinely interested in your product. You may have thought, "What is all of this? Things are going my way." That's what this divine order means. "The universe" can mean the same thing; the point is that again, we can have a sense of something larger than ourselves that interacts with us.

Marjorie Kelly observes that looking for a cause and effect relationship to such occurrences is a fundamental misunderstanding. "We are not separate. Physics teaches us that actions at a distance appear instantaneous, with no time for cause and effect. How can this be except that we are not separate? I do not 'cause' events to occur—but through meditation I align myself with the unseen order. My desires are part of that order. It is not all passive. I am aligning myself to the larger order of which I am a party and I am aligning myself to my own deepest desires. They are part of the same whole." This is why everything we do must be performed with the utmost integrity, so we align with our desires properly.

What does this mean? Are we not separate? Isn't that strange? But suspend your traditional thinking for a moment and consider the possibility. We've all had experiences like being in a room full of people and knowing that many of the people are thinking the same thing at once. But only one person verbalizes it. In the scientific community it is not uncommon for several scientists to think along the same lines in order to solve a problem. On a larger scale, international prize winners will be working on the same research path to solve a major challenge. How do we test this supposition that we are not separate? We have ways we pick up information that are common to many people.

We'll discuss this further in Chapter 14 about the Divine "unseen order" and begin to realize that our desires are not passive but what I refer to as co-creative, and that we have a partnership with the Divine to have our *needs* met, even though they may not be our *wants*.

Kathy Gardarian also reflects this entrepreneur's wholeness idea, and expands it to include the concept of the holograph:

> I believe everything is synchronicity—and therefore everything is a reflection of the same idea. All aspects are the same fundamental one thing—what you call creation or God—and it is holographic. Each contains everything; everything is all. Every separate concept is its own thing *and* its own version of the same one thing.
>
> If you are familiar with the idea of cloning, then recognize that each and every cell in your body contains information for a whole body. That is the idea. Each and every single separate concept is a different manifestation of the same one thing. Cause and effect: the same event.

For those not familiar with holographic images, remove a credit card from your wallet or purse. Look at the three-dimensional picture on the card that shines, the colors shifting as you move the card. That is a holograph. Michael Talbot, in his book *The Holographic Universe*, explains that the holographic universe is a model for us to understand our own human existence. Through a laser process, an image is etched onto a plate, and perhaps this image is of a bird. If the plate that contained the image was broken, you could take any single shard of it, project it under light, and you would see not just the tip of the wing, but you would see the whole bird again. If we expand this example into our own lives, we see that each of us holds the image of the whole, part of this first plate. We have many words for it: the universe, God, The Source, to name a few. We are a piece of the whole, but we contain the information for the whole. Every separate concept is its own thing *and* its own version of the same one thing. Marjorie frames this concept another way: "We are nodes of a much larger being."

There is another side to this, a very human one. I will share with you a story of my own experience, a reaction in the midst of reflection on the holographic universe. I had just finished Talbot's book, and was contemplating how vast, how grand this universe truly is, and I am a part of it all. How wonderfully we are all made! I closed the book and walked to the grocery store to pick up a few items. I wandered around the aisles, still thinking about how I am connected to everything, and what an amazing thing a grocery store is, bringing goods from all over the world to rest in one place. I took my armload of groceries to the cashier and came face to face with the rudest person I had experienced in a long time. She was picking up items and making comments about each item, criticizing me as she asked why I would want to buy this or that. It was like I had met my antimatter, the person expressing the exact opposite of what I was feeling. As I grabbed my bag and walked out of the store I caught myself muttering, "I'm going to pull the plug on this holographic universe!"

What do the Marjorie's, Kathy's, and my points of view have in common? It's the way we look at synchronicity through the lens of interconnectivity, seeing ourselves as pieces of the whole, but that we also carry information of the universe within us. They also point to a different way of comprehending our ties in life, suggesting that we are connected like Chief Seattle's web, even if we don't like what we are connected to, as in my story.

An exercise to more fully illustrate this connectiveness comes from a business workshop I recently attended. In the afternoon, we were to pair up and without prior discussion asked to take five minutes to think about a subject, something that we did not know much about or had very little exposure to. Car repair? Hairstyling? Cellular phones? We were then asked to come up with a short presentation, a minute or so, and just talk about this subject to our partner as if we were experts. I paired up with another person, dreading this exercise. What can I tell this other person in a minute about a subject I don't know? Is the purpose of this exercise to show me how ignorant I am?

But it showed something very different. I went first and talked about calculus. My partner then talked about history. We were to find out later that she was a mathematics major in college, and that I had a history minor. The point of this story and the point of this exercise is that we know more than we think we know. We, having our strength in each other's weakness, could confirm the fact that we each knew more than we thought about our chosen subject. This "group mind" made us aware that we are able to tap into more than we think we do. Now, if we can tap into this intelligence, group intelligence as part of our own intelligence, can we also tap into another part of the web, such as the understanding of time?

CONSIDER TIME

One exercise that I might start off with when working with new clients is a discussion about time. Each participant gets one minute to talk about their watch. Why do they wear a watch, or if not, why not? Is it digital or analog? Roman or Arabic numerals? Did the person choose it or was the watch a gift? The discussion then focuses on our relationships with time. How do I view time? Is there never enough time to do the things I want to do? Is it true that projects don't get the time that they need? Are my children or partner not getting the attention that they need, because there is not enough time?

What this discussion opens up is our relationship with time and our relationships with others who have differing per-ceptions of time. How does it influence our relationships and affect the way projects do or don't get done. It is as common to have misunderstandings over time as it is to have misunder-standings over money. Some people run on chronos time. You know that they will come to work on time, and be prompt to appointments. Others may live in their own time zone and arrive habitually late.

How does our perception of time influence synchronicity? It may seem obvious when we see a movie such as *Sliding Doors*, where a matter of seconds causes a woman to miss a train. We see the course her life takes after missing the train. We also see back and forth during the movie the course her life would take if she had a few seconds more to catch the train.

We may question times when we might have missed the train, that our awareness of time, tightly reined, didn't allow us the time to connect with other people, to reflect on clues that may have been glimmering, but we were too busy to notice. Or, we could have been passive in relating to time, not wanting to be aware of key events that happen together, acknowledging synchronicity, and valuing other people's role in it.

EXERCISES

1. Take Note of Your Dreams

   As a part of your notebook/journal, do not underestimate the power of your dreams and how they relate to your waking life. Sometimes they are disturbing, or can be taken too literally, but you need to create your own interpretation.

   Remember Mark Juarez, creator of the Happy Massager® in Chapter 7? He dreamed about his product and upon waking drew it out and pursued his dream. Mark says, "Suddenly I had a flash of inspiration which has led to the design of the product which then kept snowballing into the company that exists today."

2. Contemplate Lifecycles

   From conception, gestation, birth, life in its many forms, and death, life cycles around. Pay attention to the cycles that are in your life: the seasons, the moon, sunrise and sunsets. The purpose of this exercise is to see time in other ways. I once read a poster that challenged the reader to look at the moon every day for 29 days, to make a drawing of it, and reflect on what was experienced. To me, this is a way to inter- and inner-connect to natural cycles.

3. Tracking Synchronicities
   You can track events that happen synchronistically as part of your notebook, or you may wish to create a special notebook. The intention is to start to keep track of synchronicity and the interconnection of it in your life. You can use the following as a guide. See Table 10-1.

When we weave this web of life and understand that we are all connected, it encourages us to take a closer look at how we treat ourselves, other people, and other creatures. We cannot act without feeling its affect on us somewhere, perhaps not directly, but in its own place and time.

Table 10-1

Entrepreneur's inner thought	Outer manifestation	Inner psychic state	Consumer benefit
1. Wanting to come up with a new kind of clothing	While on a trip, found an example in a shop window in England; the organic cotton movement began	1. Wanting to change jobs	Clothing that's beneficial to the environment
2. Wanting to create an organic food business	Bought organic food, copied labels, thought of a name Shelves at stores opened up for his product	2. Wanted to earn money for school, open up a business to support that dream	High quality, great tasting food
3. Wanting to create a tool to help massage therapists who are susceptible to carpal tunnel syndrome	Dreamed about the tool, woodworker let him use his workshop after hours; later, applied for a U. S. patent, and the patent process was completed in one day	3. Sustained injuries in an accident, pursued massage for self, passionate about this aspect of healing for other people	Tool of benefit to massage therapists and enthusiasts to relieve effects of carpal tunnel syndrome

4. Wanting to build a business around a product—shoes made from recycled components	Unexpected people were willing to help her, from building sample prototypes to creating business networks. She was awarded a $110,000 grant to develop the sample run of shoes. Later, while looking for an alternate supplier of shoe fabric she was told about an expert who knew essentials of polypropylene fabric. She tried to contact him for almost a year. He turned out to be her next door neighbor's father.	4. Wanting to help recycled products find niche in mainstream clothing	Consumers have more choices for apparel in the marketplace

Table 10-1 *Continued*

Three people remarked that specific situations unfolded for them when their needs and wants were very clear. Two examples of how that inner clarity influenced the outer manifestation follow:

Inner thought	Outer manifestation	Inner psychic state	Consumer benefit
1. Want a business following four criteria: The location in X city, with X amount of square footage, with X amount of rent, and X amount of lease.	Declared this to a business partner, who within 24 hours searched for a location in X city, and within three days found a place with the exact criteria.	1. Desire to have a unique business	Spa in the center of an urban center, educational community focus
2. Worked with partner on business and marketing plan. Determined X amount was needed to start the business. Very clear on goals, knew something would happen	Entrepreneur's brother called, asked if the entrepreneur got a letter from an uncle. She said no, then went home to find a letter containing an inheritance for the exact amount of money needed to proceed with the marketing plan.	2. Determined to have a business that reflected values	Publication of interest to audience of entrepreneurs and business people

Part III

Water
Reflecting on Synchronicity

Water is reflective (no pun intended). In this part, two areas that need more are introspective time are Barriers and Ethics. To put yourself in a frame of mind to read this chapter, consider the following questions and comments:

- What do I value?
- What criticism have I encountered when I have spoken about synchronicity?
- Have there been times when I felt I couldn't act on a synchronistic experience? Why?
- When have I blocked synchronicity from happening in my own life? In other people's lives?
- What accomplishments have I felt good about in my life? Did any occur because of a synchronistic event?

Chapter 11
Taking Down the Brick Wall
Uncovering Barriers

"What's holding you back?" my mother used to call to her children when opportunities, like talent shows, contests, or running for a school office, came our way. Although it was an unwelcome question growing up, especially as a teen, it's a question all adults can use when they feel stuck in their thoughts or feel they're in a rut.

Taking down the wall a brick at a time, we'll explore what holds us back from accepting synchronicity in the business mainstream. Why are these events seen as impossibilities and sometimes even threats?

Some of the reasons synchronicity is not accepted in the mainstream can be expressed as questions: Why do I fear it? Where's the empirical evidence for it? Where is it when I want it? What is in our control? Why do I not feel worthy of these experiences? They happen all the time, why pay attention? It's puzzling; why doesn't it fit into my current understanding? Why does it feel so weird?

WHY DO I FEAR IT?

I moved to a new home. I knew that a superfund site was nearby and might have affected the property with toxins left in the soil. At the library, I asked the reference librarian if she had a map of the site. She said, "Oh yes, we do have a file on it," and walked toward the reference section to scan the shelves. I glanced down on her desk while I waited for her, and saw a map. Looking closer, I remarked, "I think this is the map I am looking for." She stopped scanning, looked at me quizzically, and walked over to the desk. Indeed, it was the map I was looking for. She looked up at me, visibly shaken. "In the three years that I have worked here, the thousands of requests I've filled, I have never had anyone ask about something that happened to be on my desk. I just can't think about this—it's too much." The librarian was shaken, upset at the possibility that perhaps something larger was at play.

Think of this in a business context. You are doing research on a site for a new building or a place to put your branch office. The research process can be very time-consuming, but synchronistic situations lend you a hand by helping you meet people, or lead you to the right book. People who are researchers, private investigators, or archivists can attest to unexpected quantum leaps in their searches.

There is a story about a woman who was researching World War II, specifically the Nuremberg trials. She was very frustrated; it seemed that the documents from the trials were not indexed well and it was nearly impossible to find what she wanted. Still, she was determined that she needed the information to finish her research. She finally said, "I'm going to find what I need right now," and pulled a book off of the shelf. She opened it to the exact document she needed.

This may remind you of the story from Chapter 2, when I was looking for my ancestors. I just said out loud, "I'm going to take the next exit off of the freeway," and stopped at the museum, which happened to be open. The genealogist on-site was working, and happened to be the right person at the right time to help me.

There can be fear in acknowledging synchronistic experiences to yourself and admitting that they do happen. If these experiences hit too close to the bone, they can be unsettling to your beliefs or values and shake what you know to be true and how things work. Information given by synchronistic experiences, if we act on it, requires us to change and accept a different way of knowing. We have to consider all that we hold close—our way of thinking, getting and processing information—and accept that we can't be in total control (although as Kathy Gardarian commented in Chapter 10, we can view a situation as being more in our control than it might at first seem). In *The Artist's Way*, Julia Cameron comments: "Answered prayers are scary. They imply responsibility, you asked for it. Now that you've gotten it, what are you going to do?"[1] The scary part is that you asked for it, now you have the benefits or the consequences of the information, depending on how you look at it. We are scared of what we don't understand. The obligation is yours, the ball is in your court, the time to act is yours, and to ignore this obligation means to allow less growth in this life. It can be unsettling to have this gift to open another part of your life.

Friends and colleagues may not share your belief in synchronicity and can't or won't understand your reasoning. "Why should I believe in this flaky thing? What proof do you have that it exists?" They will question your decision-making ability, which may lead you to doubt yourself or strengthen your resolve. So how do you counter this skepticism? You can treat it one of two ways; you can take the information and use it to your benefit and the benefit of others, or you can turn your head and walk the other way.

---

1. Julia Cameron, *The Artist's Way* (New York: Tarcher Putnam, 1992) 62.

WHERE'S THE EMPIRICAL EVIDENCE?

"It's interesting that you are doing a causal study about acausal phenomenon," a young journalist commented when I talked about this book's contents. The scientific method holds to the empirical approach to establish truth. The experience has to be repeatable. Synchronicity works outside of what we know to be true about the scientific method. It pushes the traditional meaning of causality, the law of cause and effect: if I do A, it will cause B.

One of this book's intention is to bring instances of synchronicity forward, to document its existence, and the influence it has had on other entrepreneurs, but in doing so, synchronicity defies traditional research methods. We cannot set up an experiment and duplicate it to try to prove its existence. Instead, I collected stories in my research and analyzed the commonalties and differences among them. Instead of keeping the subjects at a distance, I wanted to know them, how they think, and why these situations in life are meaningful and important to them.

One retail entrepreneur commented that, "Duplication takes it out of the sense of wonder, don't try to analyze it too much." Another entrepreneur advised, "Give synchronicity its sense of wonder, of grace . . . Just accept it when it happens."

WHERE IS IT WHEN I WANT IT? WHY DOESN'T IT ACT THE WAY I WANT IT TO?

Rainier Maria Rilke wrote about judgments needing their own time to develop, and that the gestation of ideas and events must be allowed. ". . . Not numbering and counting but ripening like a tree, which doesn't force its sap, and stands confidently in the storms of spring."[2] Nature has its own kairos time that it heeds. When pregnant women wait for labor, the days have their own time. We can't order synchronicity from a catalog, and in five to

2. Rainier Maria Rilke, *Letters to a Young Poet* (Boston: Shambala, 1984) 41.

seven business days take it into our office, open the package, unwrap the tissue, and magically have our expectations met. When we open the parcel, it is not always what we ordered, what we asked for. We may wait days or years for these things to happen—relationships we've wanted start to bud, the right business opportunity or market opens wide. It's frustrating not to know if something will be successful, and our impatience makes us doubt. We want things to happen when we demand them.

An entrepreneur commented that, "Synchronicity is life unfolding." I remember this feeling clearly after marketing at a conference. I was feeling pushed to make X many contacts, sell Y amount of product, and just felt harried after a few days. I drove to a quiet place, next to the water, centered in the middle of a bay. Sitting on a rustic bench, I pulled out my journal and started writing about how stressed I felt, how caught up in things I was. I kept writing, intense feeling becoming lines in the journal. I didn't even look up during the process. I asked for a sign of peace, something I could take back to the conference and think about when things got too intense.

I closed my eyes and sat back on the bench, letting it support me. I opened my eyes and saw the most vivid rainbow I had ever witnessed in my life. I blinked again, because there had not been a hint of color in the sky a few minutes earlier. The ends of the rainbow touched the land on each side of the bay. I heard someone behind me cooing, and I turned to see nearly a hundred people gazing at the same arc. I had not even heard them gather. We weren't in charge of the experience or the collective behavior; it happened in its own time. I had no idea what my requested sign would be—would it be a gentle, soft breeze? someone I knew sitting beside me? a cat curving its tail at my feet? And I didn't know when this sign would arrive. Would it be instantaneous? Later that night? The next day?

What I am notorious for is "pushing the river." I am impatient, and want my plans to work out in my kairos time. I push so hard at times that I am pushing against the current of a river. I am reminded of a story from Anne Lamott's, *Bird by Bird*, that explains this concept. The passage that captured me: "The gulf stream will flow through a straw provided the straw is aligned to the gulf stream, and not at cross purposes with it."[3] I think this is true for many entrepreneurs. We live with this dichotomy of hurry, hurry, hurry to prepare and then wait, wait, wait for our next direction. It's very hard on people who are close to us, our families and our employees who wonder how we can be so successful but be so fast and slow, leaving them to deal with our erraticism. Other entrepreneurs just find that their lives are always in the hurry mode, and find it incredibly hard just to take a day or two to rest every few weeks. When they do take a day off, they play as hard as they work, very intensely. This also can cause some friction.

We are also guilty of "pushing the river" in other ways. Trying to manipulate other people to conform to our sense of timing breaks up many relationships. The key is to understand each other's timing. U.S. workers who travel to different parts of the world will understand that other cultures have their own time. It can be frustrating to learn how to not push so hard that someone becomes offended and takes their business elsewhere, without becoming so unassertive and unassuming that we appear disinterested or bored.

There is the problem of letting relationships unfold, which affects both our business and our personal lives. We are watching everything going well in a sale to a customer, feeling on the crest of a wave, but we can fall if we push the timing. We negotiate a contract, need an answer by 3 P.M., and by 4 P.M. there is still no phone call. You inquire and they don't want to talk to you; all they say is that you misunderstood their contract and you are being too pushy. We can feel this in our everyday lives: When *can* the product be shipped? When *will* the bill be paid?

In marketing, there are times when a product is being launched and synchronicity is induced. You see an ad for a new

3. Anne Lamott, *Bird by Bird* (New York: Anchor, 1994) 121.

type of jeans, one that never needs ironing, doesn't fade or tear, and resists stains. It is on a billboard as you go into your office. You see advertisements in the newspaper, perhaps even an article by a product manager or a testimonial. You may receive a postcard in the mail from a local distributor for the jean. You hear a catchy jingle on the radio, espousing the benefits of the garment while maintaining that it still looks and feels great! Other people will admire your jeans and of course they come at an affordable price!

All of these modes of advertising are working in order to create excitement for the product. Perhaps this product even enters into our inner psychic space and we start noticing that we are noticing these new jeans. Is this real synchronicity or is this a false inner state?

An example of "pushing the river" from our personal lives deals with infatuation. You may be admiring someone at a distance, noting when they do this or that activity, casually noticing where they may eat dinner. You are hoping to create those times of, "Oh, I just bumped into you! You go shopping here?" when you know you are trying to set up a synchronicity for the express reason of getting someone interested in you. At one extreme you get infatuation—at the other extreme, stalking. Would I call either one of these synchronicity? No. It is a set-up.

WHAT IS IN OUR CONTROL?

Another barrier to acknowledging synchronistic experiences is the inflated ego. When a person feels that he/she has all the answers to all problems in the world (i.e., neighbor's issues or employee issues), and think they can control events is when he/she gets into trouble. It is an arrogance of knowing "nothing else exists outside of my frame of reference." We don't need to learn anything, as we already know it all, and live the illusion that we can control it all.

Yet another kind of egotism is often prevalent. This may seem like a paradox, but egotism can also be expressed when you *don't* value your own thoughts or articulate your ideas. When you are resigned to a complete lack of control, you often afflict yourself and those around you with your apathy. I call it "Ego A." The symptoms and hallmarks are different from Ego B, but the outcome is the same.

Table 11-1

	Ego A	Ego B
Symptom	shouting, stomping, and slamming	penitent, sad
Hallmark	attracts rage	attracts pity
Outcome	manipulation	manipulation

When we come from a place of either over- or underdeveloped ego, we don't operate from our authenticity. We become as false as when we set up synchronicities in the outer world (like above), only this time, it is in our inner world. When our maligned egos, for whatever reason, are functioning, our authentic selves are not engaged.

I have a technique I use with clients, usually in one-on-one sessions. I have them imagine the different parts of themselves. These could be the innocent, the child, the rowdy, the conservative, the angry one, and the parent. I ask them to think about each one of those characters, spending a minute getting into the role, really feeling it. Then I ask them who is in charge today? Is the child in the role of vice president in charge of corporate communications? the angry one assigned to chief operating officer and spewing venom today? How about the rowdy as VP of finance? Are you overspending and not caring about what you buy? In the exercise we explore the different facets of ourselves and how the hurting parts that are not working together segment us away from the parts that are working, those authentic aspects that form the center of us, from which our best work develops, opens, and blossoms.

WHY DO I NOT FEEL WORTHY OF THESE EXPERIENCES?

The antithesis of developing, opening, and blossoming is to not feel worthy of living. Like Auntie Mame, I believe a lot of us starve for many different reasons. Can we deserve the good that happens to us? Brazilian entrepreneur Tamas Makray asks, "How do we feel about the good that happens to us?" Embarrassed, Gracious, Grateful? If you want to check your answer, remember when someone complimented you either for something you did well, or complimented you just as you are? How did you feel? Did you look away embarrassed? Could you look the person in the eye, and with an authentic voice, reply, "Thank you"?

Do we feel we deserve less than being co-creators of the universe, working in partnership, neither having all the control over the outcomes nor all the answers? We'll talk more about co-creativity in Chapter 14.

THEY HAPPEN ALL THE TIME: WHY PAY ATTENTION?

Some people react to synchronicities as if they are ho-hum, run of the mill events. They wonder: "Why should I believe in or keep track of them? Why should I give thanks for them? They happen all the time, so why are they important? They're not *that* important."

A friend of mine, through a series of events that happened within a day, thought about buying Microsoft stock. He discounted the experience, then found out that within a week the stock split. I did the same thing with Edmark, an educational software developer. I had some events that happened within a day that told me that this was the time to buy Edmark stock, but I let the thought go, and within a week, the stock split. I had belittled the information and did not act on it. It seemed too commonplace, like a billboard that everyone could see and that everyone would act on.

We know from the stories in this book that synchronicity is too important to ignore. When we get these twinges of information we need to act on them. We may choose not to act toward that direction completely, or we may choose to plow full speed ahead into what we discern it means. I hope that by the end of this book you will get a full picture of why synchronicity is important. We don't have to understand it fully to see its value.

IT'S PUZZLING: WHY DOESN'T IT FIT INTO MY CURRENT UNDERSTANDING?

These events can be hard to describe. How does one believe that contained in a synchronistic experience is a lesson to be learned, or that an outer event could be related to an inner thought or dream? How does this fit into what we already know?

Psychologist Blythe Clincy made a comment about intuition that could be applied to our beliefs in synchronicity: "We may convince our students that this mode of thought is an irrelevant or indecent way of approaching formal subject matter. We do not actually stamp out intuition, rather, I think, we drive it underground."[4] I think there have been plenty of times when my belief in synchronicity has been driven underground. One time was with people who dismissed it, saying it happens all of the time, during your life you'll see how much it occurs. It's not really that big of a deal.

An issue that arises when one thinks a great deal about synchronicity is the need we have to classify everything into dichotomies of good/bad or right/wrong. We have explored classification in an earlier chapter. Sometimes we forget that synchronicities develop in their own time and have their own outcomes. What is good/right in the short term may not be seen that way in the long run.

---

4. Philip Goldenberg, *The Intuitive Edge* (New York: Tarcher Perigree, 1983) 19.

The converse is also true. This is such an important point that I am going to restate it: What we may think worked out for the best in the short term (I want a trip to Europe and I'm going right now!) may not be the best in the long term (credit card interest). The opposite occurs, too; some crummy things happened (I got fired!) that turned out to be blessings in the long run (I started my own business, which I have always wanted to do). Many successful entrepreneurs have been fired or laid off. What seems to be a bad short-term outcome turns out to be excellent for the long term. Many people in this position are free to finally follow what they really want to do, and create a business that serves their inner authenticity and serves others.

Entrepreneur and general contractor Jack Rafn of The Rafn Company explained that one of his disappointments was a bid that he didn't get, but in the long term the failure saved his company because the cost overruns of the project would have wiped him out. He also observed, "Virtually all of my greatest disappointments have become my greatest blessings. I can no longer determine what is good and what is bad based on feeling or perception."

It is a tragedy when we consider ourselves failures based on something we think turned out wrong, or our perception of wrong at any given moment. I agree with Jack's statement above—events unfold in the own time, their kairos time.

WHY DOES IT FEEL SO WEIRD?

"Some things are better left alone." How many times have we heard that expression, especially from authority figures at certain times in our lives. It's easy to refuse to delve into the meaning of experiences. At times we have been encouraged not to put energy into things that are seemingly impossible to understand or to influence. If there isn't a logical explanation already in place, why bother to try to understand it? My niece has a saying for things that cannot be explained: "It's just one of life's little mysteries."

Sometimes these events are coupled by an altered state: a feeling of floating, being surrounded by light (Jung termed this experience *numinous*). To some people it has the feeling you get when you are coming down with the flu, or having a side effect from a medication. These kinetic experiences do feel different and unexplainable because they are unusual. Some of us are not used to living in our physical bodies, we are always focused on how we think, how we learn, what new information is available, and always discerning how to proceed with a plan. But these physical feelings are a part of the experience.

Synchronicity hasn't yet found its niche in the business mainstream or, for that matter, in our lives. We have not yet developed this tool to its full advantage because we are trapped in our current way of thinking. Some people are unable to take the bricks of traditional reasoning down to create a space for synchronicity in their existence. I invite those who have a tough time considering this phenomenon to simply climb up and take a peek over the wall.

It is important to note that I do not recommend throwing caution to the wind and using synchronicity as your only tool. When you have well-developed filters to screen what is good for your path, your life, and lives of all in the world, then we are making strides in our ethical evolution. In the next chapter we'll explore the ethical implications of synchronicity, and delve into a more in-depth discussion about discernment.

EXERCISES

Are you skeptical of discussing synchronicity? with your friends? with your co-workers?

Some of the views I've had in discussion have opened up a lot of understanding between people who have different levels of beliefs regarding synchronicity. Many people have answered no to the question, that they do believe there are synchronistic events. Other people say they are absolutely skeptical, while others tell convincing stories.

Do you fear that there are some things in your life that are ultimately uncontrollable?

Most people answer yes to this question. Death is high on the list of fears, as well as the fear that they will fail in finding a life's partner and die alone. Many are afraid that they might die without having fully lived.

Have you had people in your life criticize you for paying attention to synchronistic experiences, wanting to brush them off as commonplace?

Usually there is at least one person in someone's life who has discouraged the awareness of or discussion of a synchronistic experience. It seems that it comes at an early age. When I was around age ten, someone told me that they are not that big of a deal, they happen all the time, no need to pay attention.

Do you fear thinking differently than other people?

This question seems to hit many vulnerable spots in people. This question brings up the fear of being different and being opened up to the teasing and ridiculing that we have either suffered or have seen others suffer.

Do you fear synchronicity?

Many people are more afraid of thinking differently and not being accepted than they fear synchronicity. Some people fear synchronicity because it gives a feeling of obligation, and others fear it for the physical feelings it can sometimes give.

Chapter 12

If I Don't Do It
Someone Else Will, and
They'll Make Money

Toward a Synchronicity Ethic

One of my favorite theater productions is *All My Sons* by Arthur Miller. Not only should this powerful play be read but it should also be experienced in the theater venue. Every entrepreneur, business student, and business owner should be required to view this work, preferably early in their career. Its message is as applicable today as it was when it was first performed.

Set in the early 1950s, the story centers on Joe Keller, an entrepreneur who owns a manufacturing company. He fathered two sons: the eldest, Larry, a pilot who died in World War II, and Chris, who is about to take over Joe's business. The business produced cylinder heads for airplanes during the war, and now produces household appliances and parts. Joe was in partnership with his neighbor, Herb Deever, who was found guilty of product negligence and is currently serving time in prison. Joe was also charged but was acquitted. The plot thickens as Herb's daughter Annie, once Larry's girlfriend and now Chris's, visits her old neighborhood and finds out through her brother George what really happened the day of the shipment. Was it really her father's fault or was he a scapegoat? Was Joe really innocent, or had he gotten away with this?

The final moments of the play ask the audience who and what we are responsible for in our business and personal lives? To what lengths do we go to protect ourselves, our family, and our assets for the sake of our financial security, social status, and our "face"? What are the legal standards or baselines of behavior, and how does that compare with the moral or ethical values of this life? What's the role of education in society?

We each have our own individual values and belief systems. What do our educational systems and societal beliefs have to do with Joe Keller, and his belief that to be a good father he must pass on the business to his surviving son? To him, "nothin' is bigger" than the family. What went wrong? What is our personal responsibility to the whole? Where is our essential sense of "human relatedness?"[1]

PERSONAL RESPONSIBILITY

How comfortable do we feel taking responsibility for our own lives? It can be so hard to look at our own issues. A philosopher once said (I believe it was Blaise Pascal) that we have "to live in our own rooms." It's much easier to observe the drama and trauma of others' lives and see their problems from our point of view. We explain that we could easily solve their problems if they'd only listen to us and do what we tell them to do. During my life I have overheard conversations of people talking about the latest soap opera. If Erica would only do this, and if Jeff would only do that, then they would have a good relationship. Yet it is irritating to us when we are called on our own faults, irritating to be told by someone what we should do from their perspective.

1. Arthur Miller, "What Makes Plays Endure" *The Theater Essays of Arthur Miller* edited by Robert A. Martin (New York: The Viking Press, 1978) 260.

Another variation of this is when we tell people how to live their lives or give our opinion of the incompetence of someone's life choices and transform them into a scapegoat. Scapegoating takes people away from personal responsibility. I've been both the scapegoater and the scapegoatee, and I bet most of us have been in each role at least once. It is draining, shows the worst parts of ourselves, and takes away from what needs to be accomplished. We get stuck in these roles of having to persecute someone to make ourselves and others feel comfortable. Sometimes scapegoating can occur when you are not aware of it. Other times it is so overt that it has the feeling that it's been rehearsed. In *All My Sons*, Herb Deever pays a very high price for being a scapegoat—a prison sentence, shame in the neighborhood from friends and abandonment by his family.

This leads me into a discussion of manipulation. When we try to manipulate people, we try to take their power but essentially end up giving ours away. At the root, we want so badly for something—love, acceptance, money, power, to name a few— that we will play people as pawns. I have had instances of work situations where a manager tried to manipulate other people by making others feel guilty about taking credit for something they did well; overly criticizing when she felt she was justified in doing so; and intentionally marking performance standards lower because "that is the norm around here." Employees can also manipulate managers by faking their roles while the manager is around, being compliant, taking credit for things they did not do, while slipping out the back door with product in hand. How personally responsible is that? Manipulation is a game no one wins. The manipulators continue to hurt themselves, no matter how long they are in denial. They act from their inauthentic selves, letting a role—like a Lost or Scared person—become president of the company. The victim of the manipulator usually finds out sooner or later that they are getting duped and will feel anger and mistrust.

This is a good time to discuss a critical point of synchronicity through a view of personal responsibility and manipulation. That is when the topic of inner psychic states comes up. We cannot fully determine someone's inner psychic state unless it is our own. In the examples in this book, those that are not from my own experience come from people who have told me their stories in depth. For some of them I may have only part of the story, only part of the "state." Be prudent in allowing others to know your inner self. Don't disclose your inner psychic states to everyone you meet. I have overheard people talk about their dreams openly in the hot tub or sauna, only to have their dream hacked to bits by the people there: "Are you sure you don't mean *that* park? And you walked through it with *my* husband. What are *you* doing with my husband?" Be wise about sharing your synchronistic experiences. I had a teacher who told me she never shared them, that they were among the personal items that are so powerful to her that sharing them would demean them. Others have told them like a tornado, spinning tales rapidly and not paying attention to the effects the tales will have on people. We need to use our gifts well, whichever way we choose to handle our experiences.

Entrepreneurs and other leaders value their gift of intuition and recognize that having the awareness of synchronicity also adds the responsibility to use the gift well and wisely. We've experienced leaders who have influenced the world with their gifts in a destructive manner; Hitler and Stalin are just two examples. Many destructive leaders are probably very intuitive, but it is what those leaders did with their gifts that made their choices so devastating. Leaders have responsibility to their followers and those they influence.

DISCERNMENT

One way to think of discernment is as a filter or a screen. There are many ways things are filtered: whales strain food through their baleen, the cells in our body filter nutrients, the filters in our vehicles strain out impurities in the lubrication system, a filter strains the water poured over the coffee. The reptilian part of our brain screens what enters into our consciousness. One of the keys in personal responsibility and decision making is to have a clear sense of self and to develop strong discernment skills. *Discernment* means to filter what is happening in your outer life and compare it to what is going on in your inner life—your goals, values, and feelings.

In decision making we use our values as filters. These filters are formed by the society we live in, by our culture, and by our families. We also strain our decisions, and in fact all the choices we make, through our past experiences and the experiences of others.

Discernment is your filter system, developed over a period of time and is constantly being refined. Education is one means of looking at and challenging our ethical screens. What I mean by education is not just education in the formal K-12 or higher education realms, but education comprised of lifelong learning, continuing education classes, reading, travel, and attendance at workshops. Relationships, especially intimate ones, are ways to learn about and adjust our screens. Traumas such as divorce, losing a child, disability, financial loss, or job loss can jar us dramatically enough that we suddenly reconsider our screens and find that we can adjust our values.

Family Filter   Our families have affected us and we continue to influence our families, in turn. We developed values from the people we grew up with. Some of these values have changed drastically as a result of being around different people, having different experiences, perhaps now living in different geographical areas. In what ways do we make decisions that affect our personal lives and the lives of others? What is best for the families we've created? Do you wonder what the next generation will hold as values?

Organizational Filter   Filters in organizations color our decisions. One organizational filter is the mission statement. When a decision needs to be made, the mission statement must be compared with the issue at hand. It can be likened to a coffee filter, in that coffee is the ideas that are gathered together, the water is the exterior market forces, and the filter refines only the best ideas through to make the ideal product.

Society Filter While I was writing this book I was very conscious that women have been published in the mainstream for a very short time—just over 150 years. My mother, a U.S. Army dietitian using her GI Bill educational opportunity in Geneva, Switzerland, met with officials there who laughed at her and shook their heads: "The United States lets *women* vote?" Women in Switzerland did not get to vote in national elections until 1971. Our society's filters have keep women from voting, from writing, from earning wages comparable to men. In a very recent past, women were burned at the stake and they still continue to be tortured and ridiculed because of a filter that defines women as less than men, unworthy, incapable, and threatening. The same occurs with race, class, sexual preference, religion, income, and education levels.

Spiritual Filter Our belief in God or a spiritual entity often casts us in the role of a child waiting for the care and guidance of a parent. Our parental filters and our spiritual filters interface in complicated ways and the resulting voices we hear often speak to us of "good." What is good in the long term? the short term? for the individual? for the community? for the planet? We'll discuss this further in Chapter 14.

COMPASS POINTS

People who value synchronicity will use it along with other discernment techniques for their personal growth. Examples include *wisdom circles* of the Quakers, *discernment* from St. Ignatius of Loyola, and *focusing* by Eugene Genelin. Various other people have developed these ways to structure our guidance.

Financial expert Dwight Olsen, who owns his own investment firm remarks: "I try to rely on synchronistic experiences to give me direction in both business and personal life. There is no question that we have an inner guidance system or system of beliefs that we need to listen to. A balance that if maintained will move us in the right direction. We have to be careful to know ourselves well enough to be able to tune into the synchronistic influences and avoid the counterfeit."

Here is the balance word again. We must balance our inner ledgers—one side with synchronicity and the other the inner guidance system (intuition) or system of beliefs (values awareness). Dwight is also talking about knowing ourselves well enough, which is where our authenticity kicks in and asks if something is right for you based on who you are. We must balance ourselves as beings with what we do.

HOW DO I KNOW WHETHER I SHOULD FOLLOW THIS SYNCHRONICITY OR NOT?

An entrepreneur told me about her "three in a row" idea. She was open to her life being constructed in a series and if she noticed events happening in a pattern of three in a row, then she would have a clear message of a particular decision. If I'm not to do it, then show me, was her attitude. I would add further questions to consider: Is this action suggested by a synchronistic experience apt to cause harm to anyone? Am I willing to be open and responsible for acting on my hunches—no matter the personal outcome? How do I know if these experiences are counterfeit? What do I think the outcomes will be?

Author David Whyte speaks of the *Via Negativa* in his work, *The Heart Aroused*, that whatever is not a clear yes is a no, and we should not follow it through. This may be counter to what we grew up with—that whatever is not a clear no is a yes. It only takes a few seconds to recall how many things now are coming at us, how many fax machines, computers, phones, requests for proposals, contracts to sign, invitations, articles to write. We are so bombarded that the Via Negativa seems a good discernment technique.

AUTHENTICITY

There is another component to synchronicity, and that is authenticity. All of us have a center place of themselves, a place where authenticity resides. This is the truest part of ourselves. Every person measures authenticity in their own way. My study of entrepreneurs proved to me that they were very specific about the way they used synchronicity. The successful entrepreneurs have an authentic match between their center place, their business calling, and what they stand for. Some people were very open and told me they get physical clues like a shiver or a gut response as to the authenticity of a question and decision. One person actually hears "the crunch of metal" while using synchronicity to make decisions. Another sees lights flickering. One of the people I interviewed for this book actually could hear crackles, similar to what one might hear in a fire, while making a decision.

One of the questions I have held during my life is: *Why do we give up who we are for what we want?* Why do we compromise our integrity for the sake of winning an office, buying a painting for a corporate art collection, or winning the love of a person? I saw this very clearly in the world of politics. When I ran for public office, I understood the temptation of wanting to tell people what I thought they wanted to hear. It reared itself when I least expected it—calling to be accepted, and to obtain their vote. So, I pose the question, what behavior do I allow to happen, particularly if I don't want to rock the boat or make others feel uncomfortable?

Ten years ago, I was an employee at a manufacturing company. Executive management held a meeting for the employees to discuss investments and pensions. Many of us asked questions of the investment broker who gave the presentation. Then I raised my hand and asked if any of our investments supported companies in South Africa. You could have heard a pin drop. I remember the hush in the room and the staring faces. The broker said he didn't know, but promised to look it up. People looked appalled that I had asked the question. I could hear the whispers behind open hands at the meeting and felt the sting of people avoiding me in the hall. However, later in the year, a few people came up to say that they had been concerned but didn't want to raise the question because they would look foolish or thought it was politically a bad move.

Every business you see on the street, in a catalog, on the Internet, is the result of someone having made a courageous decision to be in business. Business is composed of decision making. Should we integrate our principles and profits? What happens when we go through crisis times?

I am inspired when I read about courageous business role models like Walden Mills owner Aaron Feuerstein. After a huge fire that destroyed much of his company, he resolved to keep going, to rebuild the plant in Lawrence, Massachusetts, and to pay the employees during the reconstruction. He said, "When nobody else is standing up and doing the just and caring thing, you have to act as though you're the only one left in the world . . . I did what used to be considered normal . . . My father would never have thought of quitting, of taking the money and running. It was unthinkable."[2] I had tears in my eyes after reading this. I had just read in the paper of another major merger of two companies, one that was cutting a significant chunk of their human resources. In this day it is especially significant to praise people, who after a tragedy like a fire are going to rebuild in the same town. It is essential that we celebrate people who keep the company going to care for the workers,

2. Lynda Morgenroth, "The Making of a Mensch" *Yankee Magazine* (December 1996) 54–59.

who now have a real stake in producing a quality product. And to pay your employees during the reconstruction? I have tears in my eyes just writing this!

I am also heartened when employees become leaders in their own right and establish programs that create positive change, without waiting for a policy or direction from above. Flight attendants at a major airline, for instance, were the ones who started the recycling program at their company—and they influenced the rest of the airlines' decision to create these kinds of practices into their day-to-day business. Leaders at all levels of the organizations are in positions of building hope. One way of doing that is to influence policy.

In business history, the trend was to build an empire, then to care for the community through works of philanthropy. It was a separate function. Now we see more and more examples of businesses that combine and integrate their profit motives together with strong business principles in the community as well as to the human resources they are responsible to. They also are concerned with the full life of their products, considering where they are manufactured, what kind of waste is incurred in the process, where the product will go after its lifetime is complete, and what the impact would be on the next seven generations. These businesses combine the altruistic focus of the not-for-profit organization with a for-profit structure. The gap of altruism between businesses is narrowing due to the awakening by the entrepreneur of altruistic personal responsibility toward society. The entrepreneur has to be involved with the creation of those decisions and the acceptance of these views in society.

RESPONSIBILITY FOR FUTURE GENERATIONS

Many of us have heard of the seventh-generation principle that was started by the Iroquois Nation, whereby each action is measured by its likely outcome decades into the future. How will our decision to build this building affect the seventh generation from where we now stand? Can we make decisions about putting in water quality centers so we preserve the water that we drink and bathe in? What about the changes to a culture when we build a factory in a town or village? Do we wait for the push of regulation to make us act responsibly or do we initiate it? What are our responsibilities toward our young people? Jack Rafn wrote the following powerful statement of his responsibility toward future generations:

> I now consider all of the inner conscious processes as valid as deliberate conscious action. Those who don't incorporate these processes in their lives substantially reduce their ability to achieve their potential and are remiss in giving their children the tools to reach and enjoy their potential.

INTERPRETATIONS OF ETHICS

Most of us grew up with the Golden Rule: Do unto others as you would have done unto you. That has served us well in most situations, although an alternative would be to do unto others as they would like to be treated. We show our arrogance when we think everyone should be treated the way we wish to be treated. We may long for a day when we are appreciated on-stage by a standing ovation, flowers given to us, and people in the audience smiling and cheering. Do you know that some people would think it would be the worst punishment to be in that situation? They would rather have quiet congratulations and a gift certificate from a store or a favorite restaurant slipped to them. But how do we always know how others wish to be treated? How might we "listen" differently to discern this? Must we have to take the time to figure this out?

This reminds me of a story my sister told me of her dental assistant. She doesn't like to floss and asked the dental assistant if it was necessary, did she really have to take the time to do it. The dental assistant replied, "You only have to floss the teeth you want to keep." Is there a lesson here? Do you only care about the employees you want to keep? Only find out about them if you want to keep them, never bothering to consider the ones you think you do not like develop their skills, and grow into someone who is responsible in a personal, organizational, and social sense.

"Ethics is how we behave when we decide we belong together. When we decide we do belong together, feel the interconnectivity between us, we prosper together."[3] Ethics is how we behave truthfully, working together to build common goals, to protect our seventh generation and beyond, and to take fierce care of where we live, our employees, and our global communities.

REFLECTIONS

How have your discernment filters changed over the years?

What family filters have changed since you have reached adulthood?

Do you feel responsible for the seventh generation from now?

What conflicts do you have between the different types of filters? For example, are there times when your family filters or values clash with those in the organization? What if I am called to a critical meeting the first time my child is in a stage production? or have to cancel a family vacation because of demands at work?

How do you feel about personal responsibility and social responsibility? In the workplace, are there times when you are in a meeting and feel uncomfortable about the group needs versus personal needs? Do you notice it in other places at work?

Do you like "living in your own room"? Would you rather tell someone else what to do than to look at the remodeling that needs to occur in your own life? How does this affect you in the workplace?

---

3. Margaret J. Wheatley, Myron Kellner-Rogers, *A Simpler Way* (San Francisco: Berret-Koehler, 1996) 62.

Do you have a scapegoat as part of your team? What does it feel like to have that dynamic going on in something you are involved in? What is your role in the team?

How do I know whether or not a synchronistic event should be followed? Am I responsible for whatever road I choose?

Do I give up who I am for what I want?

Did Joe Keller feel connected to anything in this larger order? Did he come to appreciate the "unbroken tissue that [is] man and society"?[4] Did he feel connected to the generations that were to follow him (as in the seventh generation)? Later in the play we find that Joe does care deeply for his business and his son, Chris. Joe wants so much to pass on the business to his son, that he declares "nothing is bigger" than responsibility toward his family. Chris rejects his father's self-justification, though, and reminds Joe in no uncertain terms that there *are* things that are bigger; Chris says he is not the only son that Joe has, and Joe realizes that those pilots were *All His Sons*.

4. Christopher Bigsby, *File on Miller* (New York; Methuen, c1988) 68.

Part IV

Air
Regenerative Aspects of Synchronicity

How can my new awareness help me re-create my life?

This part will be divided into two chapters. The first one looks at how we have chosen our careers, our vocations. The second chapter's focus is on how synchronicity influences the way we look at our interaction with God, or whomever we consider our spiritual source. To put yourself in a frame of mind to read this chapter, consider the following questions and comments:

- Do I believe that synchronicity has played a role in my life? in my career choice?
- How has synchronicity affected different parts of my life?
- Can I believe that a Higher Power works synchronistically?
- Do I credit and thank a Higher Power when things work out?
- Whom do I admire? What are their vocations? (not necessarily what they do for a living)
- Do I feel blessed?

Chapter 13

Walking on the Path

Synchronicity Influences Vocational Choices

What did you want to be when you grew up? My childhood choices were a priest, an astronaut, and a dancer. Since there were societal gender filters for the first two occupations excluding me from those at the time, I first focused on being a dancer. As Sally Ride made her way into the space program, I watched as a part of me went up with her. I'm not an astronaut, as things turned out, and my vocational ideas have changed over the course of my life. But three strong trends have emerged: entrepreneurial ventures, consulting, and writing.

Some career advice I was given as a new college student and now give to my clients and students, was to look at my first three memories of my life. The theory was that these three memories have some impact on your career. One of my first memories was of riding a 1952 Ford tractor, sitting on Dad's lap. As a farmer, he was wearing his coveralls, dusty and streaked with grease. I must have been about three, had my hair pulled back in a ponytail, and wore a torn T-shirt and jeans. He showed me how to start the tractor—he called it "engaging the engine"—by pressing the metal button under the steering wheel and pushing in the clutch pedal. We drove up the green meadow, toward the one-room schoolhouse that my dad had attended. The sun was just setting behind the undulating Palouse hills, and my dad's bass voice asked, "Would you like to steer?" I put my tiny hands on the big wheel, while he kept one of his callused hands nearby to guide.

In this vignette I can revive the memories that influenced who I am and what my career choices have been. I learned that I had a destiny and I could drive toward it at differing speeds. It was up to me to know how to steer into the direction of that destiny. I got my intense curiosity about the way things work by watching and interacting with machines. I picked up respect for and appreciation of land, and learned that although some things, like the weather, are totally out of my control, it was up to me to engage the engine and go forward anyway.

Another early memory was of the winter my family traveled down the icy, steep, and windy Lewiston Grade to go to the central business district. After walking around the store with my mom for a while, she took me into the bookstore. She asked me if I saw a book I liked. I pointed to a cover of white, red, and green: *The Cat in the Hat Beginner Book Dictionary*. I stretched to grab it, but as I was shorter than the counter, Mom reached over, picked it up from the display holder and handed to me. I clutched it tightly against my heather wool coat, the one with the green velveteen collar. Mom had to persuade me to give it to the woman at the counter, just for a few seconds, so she could see what the price was, marked on the cover. My mom taught me to read at around age two, and that *Cat in the Hat Dictionary* was one of the tools she used. I still have it.

From my mother's influence, I brought into the life I live now that reading is key to knowledge and power. She also loved to travel and talked about the places where she had lived through the artifacts around our home: brass plates from India and a silver plate and music box from Geneva. I have an intense interest in what happens in the world and humanity's role in it.

A third memory is this: I am dancing on the front lawn of the house. It seems like I was constantly dancing then, as I do now. In the writing of this book, I frequently stopped to dance. It is my way of expression, and the steps help me choose the feeling behind the words. Dance has taught me that bodies are important to our work. Our bodies, while they are transportation vehicles, are much more than that. They hold our intelligence; we cannot just reason with our mind and neglect our physical selves.

What do all of these recollections mean in our understanding of synchronicity? I believe that our earliest experiences and our earliest memories play a role in choosing our vocations. These memories have also influenced the way my inner psychic state relates to the exterior world, and ultimately, how my awareness and my wants and needs are created in the physical world.

Do you remember an exercise in a previous chapter, where we looked at our learning and motivation styles? I asked you to look at the ways your inner psychic state developed to be in the condition it is in. One of the questions I asked was, "What were some of the influences early in your life? Look at your family, then think of neighbors, friends, school, pets and animals, and the landscape you grew up with."

People have asked me what difference the family has made, or what influence the landscape has on my development. This is where your first blueprint comes into being, the way you start learning, taking in and storing information. Our love or fear of learning starts here. Our way of interconnecting with people, nature, and thoughts and values starts here. As we begin to select our vocation, waiting for the synchronistic events to signal our way and time forward, we continually have to work within the nuances of our minds, bodies, and souls.

HOW DOES SYNCHRONICITY INFLUENCE THE VOCATIONAL CHOICE OF AN ENTREPRENEUR?

Most of the entrepreneurs I spoke with look at synchronicity in more detail from a "feeling point of view," not just intellectually. For example, when they talk about their experiences, it often includes a physical response, a feeling of warmth, or a chill up the spine. Their breathing changes. It becomes slow or rapid, and interestingly enough, they take into account their emotional states when they make a decision and the ways an emotional state can influence a choice. Entrepreneurs stress an understanding and a following of "their path" or what they felt was their chosen way, or purpose, and how they were able to align their lives and their business with these feelings.

Creator of Cafe Flora in Seattle's Madison Park District, David Foecke remarked:

> I see synchronistic experiences as things that happen when I least expect it, but that also happen more frequently when I'm following my "chosen path," whatever that means. When I feel like I am doing daily what I am "meant" to be doing, synchronistic experiences seem to happen more often. I interpret them as a sign from the universe that I'm on the right path.

Like David, several entrepreneurs see synchronistic experiences as a way to validate being on the right path, the sign they have been looking for merging the purposes of their authentic lives with their chosen vocation or business. They see synchronicity as a verification that they are going in the right direction.

Jackie Sa sees her synchronistic events as telling her that she is "Definitely on the right path and toward a most wondrous journey of self-actualization, though very painful, humbling and puzzling along the way." Jackie sees synchronistic experiences and the direction they provide as not always pleasant.

Devi Jacobs says "synchronicity is life unfolding. You know what you want but sometimes you don't know how to get it. Synchronicity is the energy that continues to move the business, life unfolding in all of its guises." As when a flower opens, we are not always in charge of when the flower will be a bud or be in full bloom. The same applies to us. We may have times we think we are in full openness, but we are not—we may think we can even predict it, but we cannot. We are taken along in a direction, until another decision pulls us away. Synchronicity can act like railroad switches, directing the cars one way or another.

SYNCHRONICITY AS A SPRINGBOARD

At times, synchronistic experiences are career—and life-changing events. The two following entrepreneurs' stories deeply connect their businesses with their lives unfolding. Their synchronistic experiences act as springboards to their life purpose. Observe what happens at the different states and the aligning of work and personal lives.

We met Mark Juarez, creator of the company Tender Loving Things, Inc. and producer of the *Happy Massager*® in a previous chapter. Mark was the one bicycling in Europe. His knee was injured, and he decided to visit a friend in Berlin. While there, they both went to a cafe, and when his friend became involved in another conversation, Mark turned to talk with a woman at the adjoining table. She asked if she could massage his knee, and he allowed her to do so. Mark says because of the experience that he had realized his calling, and he began to take classes at the massage institute. This is more of his story:

> I could soon see and feel the benefit massage had in my life, and in the lives of people I worked on. I became frustrated when carpal tunnel syndrome set in because I could not massage as many people as I wanted to. I wanted to create a tool that would allow me to give an effective massage without damaging my hands. I played with many ideas but it was an image in a dream that gave me the idea of the Happy Massager®. The next day, I created a drawing of the massage tool, gathered materials, and headed to a woodworking shop in Berlin to create the prototype. When I arrived, the woodworker was closing the shop for the day. After explaining my situation, he made an exception and let me in to drill the holes in the wood. Despite time restraints, I was able to drill the holes at the extremely precise angles needed on the first attempt. Again, synchronicity was at work when I headed to New York to

apply for a patent. Most people have horror stories regarding their pursuit of patents; however, after massaging the staff, my request was pushed through and completed by the end of the day.

Discovering Deja Shoe   Our second story comes from Julie Lewis, founder of Deja Shoe, an Oregon maker of footwear constructed from recycled materials. Julie tells how she read an article in the *Oregonian* about markets for recycled materials. She told a person at Allied Eugene Tire/Rubber company that she was thinking of making shoes out of recycled materials. The person suggested she call Bill Bowerman, founder of Nike. Julie called him and he asked her to send a sketch, but she wanted to show him the sketch in person. She came up with a design and a company name—Deja Shoe—and went to visit him. He took a great interest in her ideas, especially the use of recycled materials. He made the prototype and connected her with people at Nike. She wrote a grant and was awarded $110,000 for her sample run. Calculations indicated that she could make 5,000 initial pairs of shoes.

Julie's footwear were featured in a *Vogue* magazine article, and the Associated Press picked up the story. Unfortunately, the story misquoted Julie, saying that Deja Shoes were only available in a woman's size six. Exasperated, Julie wondered, "Now what will we do?" She called and told the writer that the shoes were available in many more sizes than size six. The writer assured Julie that amends would be made. Deja Shoe was then featured in an article in the *Wall Street Journal*.

Two other major instances of synchronicity occurred for Julie. In the first one, she was looking for a person for her management team, a person from Avia shoes. She soon found out that he lived around the corner from her, and the man's son was a friend of Julie's son.

The second instance was when Julie was ready to make the second run of shoes. Frustrated because she couldn't find another polypropylene manufacturer, she kept on the phone to find experts who could help her. Many months passed. She lamented to a neighbor about how she wanted to contact this one man that many people recommended she talk with. The neighbor replied, "Julie, the person you are looking for is my father!" What would be the statistical probability of those two things happening?

Julie and Mark both speak of how the synchronistic experience opens the awareness of how people can help you. Let's apply what we learned in Chapter 2 when we looked at synchronicity through life events and the four elements: openness, being in the present moment, vulnerability, and honesty. In Mark's case there was the openness to look at alternatives to surgery; being in the present moment at the cafe, to be able to engage with someone; being vulnerable to strike up a conversation, allowing a stranger to give him a massage; and being honest with himself about his desire to pursue his calling, his vocation.

In Julie Lewis' words: "Synchronistic experiences influenced the creation of my business and continue to influence it. Specific instances include people coming into focus that I hadn't been aware of before who could influence the business and in manifesting funding sources. The helpfulness of these contacts only became clear after I met them." And that is true—at times we don't know why we meet people—and sometimes we find out later how important they've been.

Mark Juarez said: "Synchronicity has helped me get past many barriers by creating opportunities for me to meet people who believed so much in what I was doing that I was able to overcome difficulties, rather than having situations reach a crisis level. My belief that all is possible also contributed to this ability. For example, after I had created the prototype, the people in my massage class were so encouraging, it gave me the confidence to pursue marketing the product."

We don't know all of the answers, but often we put up barriers when we fear that we don't know the answers to the situations that life presents to us. Sometimes we don't know why we meet the people we do, and only notice their effect they have on our lives until later. The answers must unfold as they do.

Our vocations reveal themselves to us, too, sometimes at the most vulnerable times of our lives, such as after death or divorce; other times we may choose a vocation out of the deep desire to improve ourselves and others; sometimes we don't know why, but we follow a synchronistic event or series of events to find that our product is something that people want or need. We can recall Craig McCaw's quote concerning the synergy of an entrepreneur's idea, the technology, and the audience. You have to accept it as it happens.

REFLECTIONS

What key experiences have I had in my life that influence what I do for a living?

Have I ever taken time out of my life to really explore what the purpose of my life is? a retreat? a vision quest? (From the Native American tradition, this is a time of prayer/meditation and fasting usually done in a natural setting. One exception I've read is in Gabrielle Roth's book, *Maps to Ecstasy*, involving a quest of sorts, what she refers to as the "Desert Experience".)

What would I do as a vocation if I didn't worry about money?

Do I take seriously my own personal mission statement?

Do I have people I know who have had interesting lives, which just seem to follow a different direction than normal people would?

I had the opportunity to work with futurist, author, and candidate for the U.S. vice presidency, Barbara Marx Hubbard. One of Barbara's concepts is that she sees vocational passion as an evolutionary change. Traditionally, the survival of our species depended on sexual arousal. Now, through evolutionary change, the survival of our species depends not only on sexual arousal but on vocational arousal. This is when we are passionate about what we do, can't wait to start another workday, are employed in meaningful positions at a living wage. How does our purpose fit into our vocation, and how does synchronicity help us? Are we willing to accept it when it happens? If we do, maybe we will eliminate some of those trips that Sisyphus had to make, rolling the boulder up the mountain.

Chapter 14

The Case for Grace
The Spiritual Aspects of Synchronicity

Dave Potter, founder of Discovery–Dialogue–Direction, was a participant in my study. Later, I was visiting the town where he lives and works and we met at a coffee shop named Vox. I wondered about the name as I went in the door. Later, I looked up the meaning of Vox, and was surprised when it was appropriately named for our discussion. *Vox* means *voice* and is the root of the word *vocation*.

As we sat in the brightly painted shop, Dave and I spoke about our calling to be entrepreneurs and the hearing and interpreting our inner voice revealing to us our life's purpose. What is our calling? What is our vocation or divine purpose at this time and place? Could it be we are all ministers and healers in whatever occupation we choose? And is synchronicity one way the universe conspires with us to bring forth our purpose?

In this chapter we focus on the spiritual realm of synchronicity and how entrepreneurs interact with the spirit and forms of creation. We'll cover the ideas of grace and divine intervention, or as Oprah Winfrey calls it, "the Hand of God."

Many of the entrepreneurs I encountered and others I interviewed give credit to a spiritual source, using words such as:

God, the Divine, Spirit. Whichever term makes you feel more comfortable, use it. I am reminded of Wayne Dyer, who said during his lectures, if you are uncomfortable calling God *God*, or *Source*, or the *Divine*, just call her Louise.

Entrepreneurs hold many personal definitions for the graced experiences of synchronicity they have had. An East Coast entrepreneur described synchronicity as "a blessing of the universe, uplifting my faith, reminding me there is more." David Foeke said of the spiritual aspect of synchronicity: "It felt like there was 'someone else out there' directing things when we were starting the business," which gives us an idea of the spiritual aspect, without crediting it a specific source. Dwight Olsen said, "I cannot help but mention the role that God plays in my life in this regard. He uses circumstances, people, and my prayer and thought to create experiences in my life." Dwight credits God directly for the role of synchronicity. All three definitions are helpful, and all point to this Divinity. It shows us the different ways that people think of the Divine, from Dwight's specific credit to God, to talking about it as a blessing, to suggesting there is "someone else out there."

I wanted a middle-ground word to use in our discussion, something that could be as inclusive as possible without muddying up the water and losing the point, so I chose to use the Divine or Divinity. My definition of this term is something that is God or Godlike or just supremely good. It's a benevolent entity that is in the world to spur our growth, to assist us, to protect us.

What if you don't think the spiritual world has a part in synchronicity? What if spirituality does not seem to influence you? What I can say to you is just keep open to this idea. If you still think it doesn't influence you, consider that you already know people who do believe in this influence, and, at the very least, you will get to know their point of view.

Let's review what we talked about in Chapter 1. I'll bring in three areas from that chapter to remind you of the ground we have already established in our discussion of synchronicity:

Jung's definition, the grace definition we had in discussing semantics, and our definition. Jung's definition of synchronicity said that synchronicity was *the meaningful coincidence between an "inner psychic state" and an outward physical manifestation or event.* The grace definition said that synchronicity defies all logic and probability and produces something surprising, or against all common acceptance, like a spontaneous healing of a disease. It includes the concept of divine intervention as the working of a higher power or divine source that intervenes in our affairs to assist us, many times in ways we do not expect. At times, we can feel other people are acting as benevolent people looking out for our best interests. Our definition said that "synchronicity is an event or series of events when the external and internal worlds affect each other, making meaningful experiences that change our lives."

All three definitions emphasize the inner psychic state or inner world. This is where we hold our concepts of the Divine. If we have the basic framework, and picture our universe captured in a painting, we may see chaos, destruction, the sun, or the green earth. We may see that the Divine has created all of these things for us. Our perceptions and recognition of the Divine are held by that inner state. We may believe that the Divine gives us everything that we need, and everything comes from the Source. Depending on our beliefs, we may believe we have no control of whether synchronicity happens or not, or we may think we have some influence. I can share with you my view of how synchronicity happens to me in a spiritual sense, and that is through the concept of co-creativity.

CO-CREATIVITY

Think of a safe deposit box. You have a key and the Divine has a key and both of you open this box, this box of your life, together. To me, co-creativity means working in partnership with the Divine. This means a pattern of give and take, where there is a deep interest in keeping the partnership going, and that

you both work through any challenges and conflicts. I am aligning my will with that of the Spirit. I do not always get what I
intend or what I think I want because there are more factors than
what I can control.

I first heard this quote when I was reading a book by Barbara Marx Hubbard. She expressed her thoughts on co-creation
this way: "The Creation is continuing and we are a part of it. We
are the womb of the future, the co-authors of Creation. Our
destiny is to share with the Creative Intention, to make more
responsibility for this Intention. As our awareness of it grows,
we are becoming co-creators."[1]

This may be a stretch for some who believe that God holds
all the strings: the purse strings, the strings that hold us captive
as marionettes, the ties that bind us together. I used to think
that perhaps I was an anomaly, that at certain times of my life,
my friends prayed desperately to know God's will, while I
prayed for a relationship with God. It wasn't until much later
that I read another quote that had meaning to me. It comes from
theologian Martin Buber, author of *I and Thou*: "You need God, in
order to be—and God needs you, for the meaning of your life."[2]
To me, that was freeing from what I thought I should believe,
based on what others told me I should believe.

How do we know the Divine is listening to our prayers or
the prayers of people and other beings around the world? Why
is there such brokenness? How can we feel whole again? If part
of being aware of synchronicity is wholeness, how can we be
redeemed? How can we mend ourselves?

SEPARATION AND WHOLENESS

Our greatest deterrent to wholeness is separation. We separate
from ourselves, our families, our relationships, our Divinity, the

1. Barbara Marx Hubbard, *The Evolutionary Journey* (San Francisco: Evolutionary Press,
1982) 3.
2. Martin Buber, *I and Thou, Second edition* (New York: Charles Scribner's and Sons, 1958)
82.

environment that sustains us, and from people in lifestyles and traditions that are different from our own. We create and force leaders to carry our agenda, the agenda of comfort in the midst of chaos. Our salvation lies in healing our separation. To heal and make ourselves whole requires us to look deeper inside ourselves and be willing to mend our wounds and divisions from others. This is not to say that we can heal everything or that we can control the way we want it resolved. Sometimes it is not possible to heal people who hurt us badly or who don't want to forgive us. But we must come to terms with and be at peace with these wounds. Sometimes it is not possible to mend issues directly.

Separation from Ourselves   When we don't reflect on what is going on in our lives, we open ourselves up to further hurt and separation. When we don't take the time to discern what we really want, we fall into negative habits. One of the most critical ways entrepreneurs separate is in self-sabotage. Once an entrepreneur is ready to build a business and gets to the point of securing funding, hiring employees, and developing a great product or service, very often something seizes up in the entrepreneur's mind. It doesn't have to be conscious. The visionary can sabotage in many ways: by building a business too quickly, by making poor decisions, or by turning away from employees and investors. This may come from a deep-seated belief that we are not worthy or can never be successful. The strong, inner machinations start to slow down or simply fall away.

The origins of the word *sabotage* are interesting. The French word for shoe is *sabot*. When factory workers became disgruntled, they would throw their shoes into the gears of the large machines to slow or damage the machines.

The tragedy of sabotage is that it can be subtle because of our focus solely on the outside world. Another tragedy is that if it goes too far, the entrepreneur drags not only himself down, but others who have invested in the dream.

Separation from Our Families   In an ideal world, our families are a constant source of strength and support. But sometimes we are born into families of origin that may not be healthy and we carry that into the families we create. One of the most essential transitions we need to make is the one into adulthood and coming to peace with our own family of origin. Joseph Campbell talked about the need for a ritual of adulthood where we formally and ritually take the reins of responsibility for our own lives.

Often, we separate ourselves from the families we create by addictions, like workaholism, that take us away from the family and distances our intimacy with others. This disregard for balancing work and families is a chronic wound that must be healed. I once asked a public official about issues of balancing work and life. I asked about this topic after other people had asked his opinion about education, health care issues, and the economy. He looked and admitted that he was astonished that I would ask such a thing. I have asked that question of many government and business leaders since then, all with varying answers, but it is a key issue, and one that most people dodge.

Separation from Our Organizations   We feel separation from our organizations in several ways:

Our hopes and dreams for making a difference lay stagnant due to the acceptance of mediocrity and the overwhelming number of meetings we are required to attend.

A merger happens, causing two value systems to clash and putting employees at the mercy of the third, and as yet unknown, culture being created.

We experience a betrayal of trust, perhaps even by a close associate.

A long-time employee becomes disillusioned about the changes the company is making.

An employee is turned down for a promotion.

All of these situations are real, and when hope is abandoned, apathy and separation replace it. We separate when we feel we cannot be a part of what is unhealthy.

Separation from Our Communities

Symptoms of separation from community may include a general pessimism about everything. We start disengaging, not wanting to vote or participate in the community in any capacity because we feel that bad things are going to happen no matter what we do. We feel that the land will be destroyed and only those with money will win, in any case. We feel that noise will only increase, that values will go down the drain, and there is no stopping it. We no longer see hopeful connections with people. We start interpreting and misinterpreting groups of people based on hearsay. For various reasons, we separate ourselves from the community that once nurtured us.

Separation from the Environment That Sustains Us

Charles Lindbergh, in his *Autobiography of Values* related a story of meeting the Masai people in Africa who told him: "We believe God is in everything. We believe God is in the trees, in the sky, the mountains, the grasses. We sing songs to the mountains and the trees because God is in them."[3] What sort of decisions might we make if we believed, as so many indigenous people do, that our Divine Source is present in everything around us? Terry Tempest Williams, who also wrote about the Masai, describes a young child, who when being punished "falls to the ground and clutches a handful of grass. His elder takes this gesture as a sign of humility. The child remembers where the source of his power lies."[4] When we make decisions that keep us from sustaining our environment, we are depleting our futures.

3. Charles Lindbergh, *Autobiography of Values* (New York: Harcourt Brace Jovanovich, 1977) 276.
4. Terry Tempest Williams, *An Unspoken Hunger* (New York: Vintage Books, 1994) 12.

Separation from the Divine   A key separation from our Divine Source, is thinking we can do everything ourselves. We continue to separate ourselves from this Source when we treat people unfairly, when we do not use our talents well, when we do not ask for what is ours, and when we separate from the rightful use of our strength. When we engage in any of these things, we continue to separate from our own wholeness and from our awareness of synchronicity.

WHAT WE MOST VALUE IS WHAT HAS WOUNDED US MOST

When we look closely at our brokenness, our wounds, we discover that there is a relationship between what we hold as our values and what we've been most wounded by. For example, think of a key value such as trust. If I have been wounded by someone, perhaps a teacher, and I still carry that scar, I will embrace trust as one of my top values, and hold high regard for people who are trustworthy. If I have been wounded by an abuse of power, I will hold power in high regard.

MERGING OF CO-CREATIVITY AND GRACE: THE OMEGA POINT

Pierre Teilhard de Chardin, a Jesuit priest, paleontologist, and prolific author of such books as *The Phenomenon of Man* and *The Divine Milleu*, wrote about the concept of Omega Point, a place in space and time when all will converge. When we can't manage to heal our wounded situations, I believe co-creativity and grace can converge to become a healing force. Theologian Paul Tillich writes: "Grace strikes us when we are in great pain and restlessness. It strikes us when we feel that our separation is deeper than usual, because we have violated another life, a life which we loved, or from which we were estranged."[5]

5. Thomas More, *Education of the Heart* (New York: Harper Collins, 1996) 254.

Grace, intellectually defined, is a freely given, unmerited favor and the love of the Divine operating in human life to regenerate or strengthen. Occurrences of grace act like a battery to charge and regenerate us to the challenges we face in our lives. Grace is freely bestowed, just like a gift.

LEADERS AND PROTECTION

One of the gifts that grace provides is protection. Leaders need protection not only from the people they sense are their enemies, but from their followers, their promoters, their own mind at times, and even, sometimes, from their friends. Larry Dossey, author of *Be Careful of What You Pray for, You Just Might Get It* said, "No one is helpless against the negative intentions of others. Methods of protection are real, powerful, and freely available." He relates a story of a Native American shaman, who, when asked how he protected himself from evil, said, "Have you heard of the Lord's prayer? Do you remember the words, 'Deliver us from evil?' You white people have one of the best prayers of protection and you don't even know it. Why I even use it myself! he added with a grin."[6]

Protection is something that you depend on from something larger than you are. Entrepreneur Jack Rafn remarks, "I see them as spontaneous events that protect the company from unforeseen disasters and guide or advance the company in the direction of dreams, goals, and prayers." In Celtic spirituality, a form of spirituality that is currently undergoing a renaissance, the *lorica* was a prayer of protection. Possibly the most famous is "The Deer's Cry" also known as St. Patrick's breastplate.

I arise today
through the strength of heaven
light of the sun
radiance of the moon

6. Larry Dossey, *Be Careful of What You Pray for, You Just Might Get It* (San Francisco: Harper San Francisco, 1997) 195–197.

splendor of fire
speed of lightning
swiftness of the wind
depth of the sea
stability of the earth
firmness of the rock.[7]

I arise today
through God's strength to pilot me
God's might to uphold me
wisdom to guide me
eye to look before me
ear to hear me
word to speak for me
hand to guard me
way to lie before me
shield to protect me
hosts to save me
from the snares of the devil
from everyone who desires me ill
afar and near
alone or in a multitude[8]

You can write your own lorica, your own protection prayers or meditations. They can be said before a meeting, a press conference, a presentation. You can also pray for the protection of the other person before a performance review, before you walk into an office with a "see me" note, before a dentist appointment. I know an entrepreneur who uses a lorica when she visits people in the field as part of her job.

Identify your vulnerabilities so that you do not have to overprotect yourself. Find people around you who have strengths to complement the areas where you feel you need more growth. Also find people who disagree with you, to make you see your own mistakes. At the other end of the pendulum, also find people who will support you, pick you up, but not overprotect you.

7. Caitlin Matthews, *The Celtic Book of Days* (Rochester, VT: Destiny Books, 1995) 22.
8. John O'Donahue, *Anam Cara* (London: Transworld Publishers, 1997) 167.

CHECKS AND BALANCES

Educator Parker Palmer writes, in *To Know As We Are Known*, about the checks and balances in the spiritual life. My interpretation, based on his writings, is outlined in these three areas: *prayer*, to feel the direct experience of the Source; *reading*, to understand intellectually the experiences of others; and in *community*, where we can test our ideas and visions and measure our growth. All are important to gain information about our spiritual journey. I look to prayer not as I had been taught, which had an emphasis on talking, but as a dialogue. I listen as much as I ask. It is a place where intuition also resides, along with direction and alignment. With reading, I get to use my powers of reasoning, memorizing, thinking. In community, I get people to help me when I need it, protect me, and challenge me to be the best person I can be. I can also talk with them if I need advice.

QUESTIONS/REFLECTIONS

1. Do I feel connected to what I consider the Divine?
2. What parts of my life do I feel separate from?
3. Do I believe that what I value is what I have been most wounded by?
4. Do I feel the need to be protected? Is that one of the roles I give the Divine?
5. Reflect on this quote from author and businessman James Autry: "Yet I do believe that our work daily gives us our best opportunities to look for the best—the Divine—in others and to manifest the best—the Divine in ourselves."[9]

---

9. James Autry, *Confessions of an Accidental Businessman* (San Francisco: Berrett-Koehler, 1996) 35.

Conclusion

WHY SHOULD WE CARE: SYNCHRONICITY'S IMPACT

On my desk is a collection of things that are meaningful to me. As you look at my desktop, you can draw conclusions about me. I have my grandmother's sewing box, a stone gathered from my cousin's lookout tower, oyster shells, a cube puzzle, a gift from my sister-in-law, a Happy Massager® from Mark Juarez's company, a leopard toy, a shell, a heart, and a barometer. I have a multicolored wooden block, a device invented by industrialist Robert Owen that provided a way of improving behavior of an employee, at a time when it was common to physically punish employees. I have a copy of Rilke's *Letters to a Young Poet*, and fragrant lotions.

- The old sewing box represents construction of an item, or to repair something.
- Oyster shells bring the memories of the natural world that we discussed in Chapter 5.
- The cube speaks volumes about the paradox of the separateness and wholeness that it is part of a puzzle.
- The Happy Massager® reminds me of the resiliency of entrepreneurs, the ability they have to go out and do what

they feel needs to be done to have benefit for themselves
and others.
- A barometer measures pressure, a symbol of the pressure
  that people have in their lives and the balance it takes to
  make the pressure bearable.
- Owen's cube reminds me of treating a company's human
  resources with dignity and respect.

Remember the boss who said to his new employee on his first
day at work, "Your job is to do your best. Mine is to remove
obstacles that keep you from doing your best." I hope that in
reading this book, I have removed obstacles from your path
toward understanding synchronicity. It is a complex subject
with many facets, many objects on the desktop to look at and to
ponder.

I hope your mixture of earth, air, fire, and water, our elements of synchronicity, has developed into a beautiful work of
art that has the ability to be articulated to others in meaningful
ways, and manifest itself in ethical ways, considering your vocation and awareness of co-creativity. What we do with the mani-
festations is up to us, but our individual decisions affect the
future of the rest of humanity and the natural world. We are
responsible for the things that we create and their effects in
this world.

The impact of synchronicity can be enormous. "Extraordinary people display calling most evidently. Perhaps, too, they
are extraordinary because their calling comes through so clearly
and they are so loyal to it. They serve as exemplars of calling and
its strength, and also of keeping faith with it's signals."[1] Ira
Progoff once said: "One specific hypothesis that is worth inves-
tigating is whether the lives of those individuals who can be
classified as 'creative persons' show a particular tendency toward the occurrence of synchronistic events. If this turns out
to be verified in any degree, the implications may be of great

1. James Hillman, *The Soul's Code: In Search of Character and Calling* (New York: Warner
Books, 1996) 28.

importance."[2] Why are the implications of great importance? As Jack Rafn said, "We harm our children when we do not give them the tools that can help them."

Synchronicity can be one of the tools that helps us, that can lead us to our strengths, which in turn will help us to better care for ourselves, our companies, our community, and our environment. It can empower us to make the connection between the inner thought and the possible outward manifestation of that thought. It can harness our strengths and ameliorate our lives. We can see synchronicity as a coincidence or as a hope to believe in. The choice or chance is yours.

To end this book, I would like to close with a story about meeting Mary Kay Ash, founder of Mary Kay Cosmetics. Several months before entering my doctorate studies, I wrote to several people—entrepreneurs, business executives, artists, writers, creative people in general—asking them for their opinions about a book subject that had to do with intuition. From their opinions, I would start to formulate a dissertation study based on what was on the minds of intelligent, successful people. Many people responded, and some people even called. I received a message from Mary Kay Ash's public relations firm. They asked if I wanted to talk with Mary Kay in person or in a telephone interview. I thought to myself, in person of course! But I wasn't sure how I was going to get there.

At that time, I was just finishing several projects, and was asked to be a witness at my best friend's wedding. My last day at a client's was Friday, and I was to leave the next Wednesday for Indiana, where the wedding would be. I was wondering how I would get everything done. After checking my calendar, I called the PR firm back and told them that I would like to speak with Mary Kay in person. I would call them back after I had made arrangements for the wedding travel.

I hung up the phone from the PR firm, then called the travel agent's office. I told them I wanted to go from Seattle to India-

---

2. Ira Progoff, *Jung, Synchronicity, and Human Destiny* (New York: Julian, 1973) 168.

napolis. The agent listed several options on different days, then said the best option would be to route me through Dallas. I knew that was my cue! I remained open, even though I did not have all of the information I needed as to how I was going to go from the airport to interview Mary Kay in her office, but I knew that something was up when I "happened" to be routed that way. I called the PR firm back, informing them of my arrangements, but I didn't hear back from them. I left several messages, including one the day before I flew to Indianapolis.

I still hadn't heard from them when I checked my messages at the Dallas airport. I decided to take a risk, to keep going, and hope that things would work out. I dialed the PR firm and got the contact on the phone. I told him that I was in the Dallas airport, that I hadn't heard from him, and that I had a four-hour layover. Would it be possible to still meet with Mary Kay, to talk with her? He told me to stand by the phone, he would call me back in five minutes. When he called back he said, "Grab a cab and go directly to her office." I ran down the corridor, jumped into a cab, and put everything together for the impending visit. I went into the lobby and waited until I was able to go upstairs and meet Mary Kay in her office. I was allotted one half hour, and after an hour, we concluded our visit. I was able to grab a taxi back to the airport and walked through the jetway as the final call was announced.

Had I not taken the risk and drawn on my perseverance reserve, to call from the airport, even though I might have been rejected, laughed at, or hung-up on, I would have not gotten the interview. But what I did receive was a wonderful hour-long conversation with Mary Kay, which set a direction that influences me yet today.

Twelve Things You Can Do to Be Aware of Synchronicity

1. Think, notice, discuss
2. Resolve, keep going
3. Check your intention, know what you want
4. Reach out, interconnect
5. Be in and with the natural world
6. Think about Divinity (Louise)
7. Read about people who think differently than you do
8. Be grateful for what you have
9. Dare to be a pathological optimist
10. Love people
11. Heal the separations in yourself
12. Enjoy the journey

Appendix of Exercises

AWARENESS OF ENERGY

When do you seem to have the most energy during the day? This is a specific exercise that will allow you to reflect on high-energy times and low-energy times and how to make better use of the times when you think clearly and those when you might need to take a break. Chapter 5.

AWARENESS OF SENSES

How does this affect you in your workplace? Being aware of your surroundings makes it easier to pick up on the clues that make you aware of opportunistic openings. Chapter 7.

CHRONOLOGICAL CHART

Make the chronological chart of your successes and reflect on the years when they happened and the turning points. Would you change any of these if you could? What have been your most valuable contributions? Chapter 8.

CHRONOLOGICAL CHART FEEDBACK

Take the same chart and share with other people who can give you honest feedback. How did your decisions affect their lives? Chapter 8.

CLEAN HOUSE

Like cleaning a room in your house, it is necessary to clean your mind of unwanted or not useful memories. If you clear out the clutter, the advantage is that you have time and energy to take action on your thoughts—immediately! Chapter 9.

COMPLETE YOUR INCOMPLETES

When you clean out a room, or clean out your mind, you are creating room for something more, something different, to take its place. You may decide to let go of projects, renegotiate, or let others complete them. Chapter 9.

CONTEMPLATE LIFECYCLES

From conception, gestation, birth, and death—life in its many forms—seasons cycle around. Pay attention to the cycles in your life: the seasons, the moon, sunrises, and sunsets. Chapter 10.

CREATING CLARITY

Take a piece of paper, and instead of writing at the top of the page, turn it $\frac{1}{8}$th of a turn so you are writing in the corner. Ask, "What do I want," write down the answer, and turn the page a quarter turn to the next corner, where you will write a different answer to "What do I want?" Keep turning the page and writing, making an inward spiral. Chapter 6.

FLASH CARDS

I may write down a list of around 40 words, then narrow the choices to ten words that I can memorize. They have to have deep meaning to me, and have to do with my focus and intention for that year. Reading the words every morning jump starts my day. Chapter 6.

"IT'S ALWAYS SOMETHING."

If you find yourself resigned to the cliché, "it's always something," try catching yourself and changing that to say, "it's always something—good." Chapter 6.

KEEP A JOURNAL

I use this to reflect about my business, to see what I did well, and places I need to improve. I also use it as a way to look into the future, or simply to mull over some problems, or reflect on a newspaper article which may impact my business positively or negatively. Chapter 5.

KNOW YOURSELF

How well do you know things about yourself that help you in your everyday life? What is the best way you learn? Do you work best under the pressure of a deadline? Are you a person who needs to have things in order before you can begin? Do you need to plot your progress, take a step at a time? Chapter 7.

LIFELONG LEARNING

Develop lifelong learning skills, curiosity, and passion for learning. We constantly have to keep updated on new procedures, ways of doing business, the influx of regulations. Chapter 8.

MULTICULTURAL AWARENESS

Take time to travel, meeting local people along the way, and cultivate friends from different cultures. Chapter 5.

NOTE YOUR DREAMS

Do not underestimate the power of your dreams and how they relate to your waking life. Chapter 10.

PAY ATTENTION TO THE NEXT 24 HOURS

From the moment you read this, be aware of what happens to you in the next 24 hours. Think of and write down an idea. Attend to intuitive voices inside of yourself. Chapter 9.

PEER AND MENTOR COMMUNITIES

These people can push you to higher heights, help you solve problems, keep you aware of developments in the workplace, and recognize when you are working against yourself. Chapter 8.

PERSONAL MISSION STATEMENT

A personal mission statement is a declaration, similar to a corporate mission statement. It clarifies who you are, your values, and the direction in which you want your life to be going into a succinct package. Chapter 6.

RENEW YOURSELF

Take vacations and times of renewal. Leaders must take time out to be competent, to listen, to not burn out. Chapter 8.

TEN COMMITMENTS

A twist to the mission statement, creating a policy is to create what I call the "ten commitments." These are a list of commitments to yourself, or yourself and others, that you feel strongly about. Chapter 6.

TIME IN THE NATURAL WORLD

Being in nature is another way to open creative space. Not only does it get your mind and body into a different place than you normally work in, but you also work with your senses differently, allowing your mind to think in unusual patterns. Chapter • •.

TRACKING SYNCHRONICITIES

You can track events that happen synchronistically as part of your notebook. The intention is to start to keep track of synchronicity and the interconnection of it with the rest of your life. Chapter 10.

TWO OBVIOUS THINGS

First, to develop positive thinking skills and goal-setting savvy, spend time with and be mentored by people who are optimistic and excellent goal setters. Second, read biographies and autobiographies for inspiration. Learn what other people did when they were feeling overwhelmed, made mistakes, and kept on going toward their goal. Chapter 6.

WRITE TO ME!

Write to me about your experiences, synchronicity and these exercises: P.O. Box 2133, Vashon Island, WA 98070, or email: satori@wolfenet.com. Chapter 9.

Bibliography
Sources by Subject

Asterisk (*) denotes sources used in the text.

SYNCHRONICITY

Aziz, R. *C. J. Jung's Psychology of Religion and Synchronicity*. Albany, NY: State University of New York Press, 1990.

*Bolen, Jean Shinoda. *The Tao of Psychology: Synchronicity and Self*. New York: Harper & Row, 1979.

Combs, A., and M. Holland. *Synchronicity: Science, Myth and the Trickster*. New York: Paragon House, 1990.

Cousineau, Phil, editor. *Soul Moments: Marvelous Stories of Synchronicity—Meaningful Coincidences from a Seemingly Random World*. Berkeley, CA: Conari Press, 1997.

Halberstam, Yitta, and Judith Leventhal. *Small Miracles: Extraordinary Coincidences from Everyday Life*. Holbrook, MA: Adams Media Corporation, 1997.

Hopcke, Robert. *There Are No Accidents: Synchronicity and the Stories of Our Lives*. New York: Riverhead Books, 1997.

I Ching or The Book of Changes. Wilhelm, W. Translator, C. G. Baynes. Princeton, NJ: Princeton University Press, 1950.

*Jaworski, Joseph. *Synchronicity: The Inner Path of Leadership*. San Francisco: Berrett-Koehler, 1996.

*Jung, Carl G. *Synchronicity: An Acausal Connecting Principle*. Princeton, NJ: Princeton University Press, 1960.

Kammerer, P. *Das Gesetz de Serie*. Stuttgart Berlin: Verlags-Anstalt, 1909.

*Kersal, Dan. Workshop booklet from Mirrors of the Soul Workshop, Seattle, WA: April 1995.

Koestler, Arthur. *The Art of Creation*. New York: Macmillan, 1964.

*——. *The Roots of Coincidence*. London: Hutchinson, 1972.

Mansfield, Victor. *Synchronicity, Science and Soul-Making*. Chicago: Open Court, 1995.

*Mindell, Arnold P. "Synchronicity: An investigation of the unitary background patterning synchronous phenomenon. (A psychoid approach to the unconscious)." Cincinnati, OH: Ph.D. dissertation, Union Graduate School, 1976.

*Pauli, W. *The Influence of Archetypal Ideas on the Scientific Theories of Johannes Kepler: The Interpretation of Nature and the Psyche*. New York: Pantheon Books. Copyright by The Bollingen Foundation, 1955.

*Peat, F. David. *Synchronicity: The Bridge Between Matter and Mind*. New York: Bantam, 1987.

*Progoff, I. *Jung, Synchronicity and Human Destiny*. New York: Julian, 1973.

Richo, David. *Unexpected Miracles: The Gift of Synchronicity and How to Open It*. New York: Crossroad Publishing Company, 1998.

*Spangler, David. *Everyday Miracles: The Inner Art of Manifestation*. New York: Bantam, 1996.

*"Synchronicity" (audio recording). The Police, A&M Records, 1983.

CREATIVITY

Bohm, D., and F. D. Peat. *Science, Order and Creativity*. New York: Bantam, 1987.

*Cameron, Julia. *The Artist's Way: A Spiritual Path to Higher Creativity*. New York: Jeremy P. Tarcher/Putnam, 1992.

Csikszentimihalyi, Mihaly. *Flow: The Psychology of Optimal Experience*. New York: Harper & Row, 1990.

*Goleman, David, Kaufman, Paul, and Michael Ray. *The Creative Spirit*. New York: Plume, 1992.

Harman, Willis, and Howard Rheingold. *Higher Creativity: Liberating the Unconscious for Breakthrough Insights.* Los Angeles: Jeremy P. Tarcher, Inc., 1984.

Mackenzie, Gordon. *Orbiting the Giant Hairball: A Corporate Fool's Guide to Surviving with Grace.* New York: Viking, 1998.

*O'Connell, Nicholas. *At the Field's End.* Seattle: Madrona Publishers, 1987.

*Roth, Gabrielle. *Maps to Ecstasy.* San Rafael, CA: New World Library, 1989.

*Soleri, Paolo. *Arcosanti: An Urban Laboratory?* Mayer, AZ: The Cosanti Press, 1993.

ENTREPRENEURSHIP

*Burke, James. *Connections 2.* New York: Ambrose Video, 1994.

*Chappell, T. *The Soul of a Business.* New York: Bantam, 1993.

*Collins, James C. and William C. Lazier. *Beyond Entrepreneurship.* Paramus, NJ: Prentice-Hall, 1992.

Drucker, P. F. *Innovation and Entrepreneurship: Practice and Principles.* New York: Harper & Row, 1985.

*Hawken, Paul. *Growing a Business.* New York: Simon & Schuster, 1987.

*Hilton, Conrad. *Be My Guest.* Englewood Cliffs, NJ: Prentice-Hall, 1957.

*Kawasaki, Guy. *Selling the Dream.* New York: HarperCollins, 1991.

Kent, C. A., D. L. Sexton, and K. H. Vesper. *Encyclopedia of Entrepreneurship.* Englewood Cliffs, NJ: Prentice-Hall, 1982.

*Krueger, Martin H. *Entrepreneurial Vocations.* Atlanta: Scholars Press, 1996.

*Kupfer, Andrew. "Craig McCaw Sees an Internet in the Sky." *Fortune,* May 27, 1996.

*Lager, Fred "Chico". *Ben & Jerry's: The Inside Scoop.* New York: Random House, 1994.

*Mariotti, Steve. *The Young Entrepreneur's Guide to Starting and Running a Business.* New York: Times Books, 1996.

*Roddick, A. *Heart and Soul.* New York: Crown, 1991.

*Schultz, Howard, with Dori Jones Yang. *Pour Your Heart Into It: How Starbucks Built a Company One Cup at a Time*. New York: Hyperion, 1997.

*Wenner, Paul. *Garden Cuisine: Heal Yourself and the Planet Through Low-Fat Meatless Eating*. New York: Simon and Schuster, 1997.

*Whiting, Bruce George, and G. T. Solomon. *Key Issues in Creativity, Innovation, & Entrepreneurship*. Buffalo, NY: Bearly Limited, 1989.

*Ziegler, Mel, Bill Rosenweig, and Patricia Ziegler. *The Republic of Tea: The Story of the Creation of Business, as Told Through the Personal Letters of Its Founders*. New York: Currency Doubleday, 1992.

MILLER

Bigsby, Christopher, *File on Miller*. New York; Methuen, c1988.

Miller, Arthur. *All My Sons*. New York: Reynal & Hitchcock, 1947.

Miller, Arthur. "What Makes Plays Endure" *The Theater Essays of Arthur Miller* edited by Robert A. Martin. New York: The Viking Press, 1978.

INTUITION

Agor, W., editor. *Intuition in Organizations: Leading and Managing Productively*. Newbury Park, CA: Sage, 1989.

*Goldberg, Phillip. *The Intuitive Edge*. Los Angeles: Jeremy Tarcher, 1983.

Noddings, Nell and Paul Shore. *Awakening the Inner Eye: Intuition in Education*. New York: Teachers College Press, 1984.

Rossman, J. *The Psychology of the Inventor*. Washington, DC: Roberts, 1931.

*Rowan, Roy. *The Intuitive Manager*. Boston: Little, Brown and Company, 1986.

Vaughan, Frances. "Varieties of intuitive experience." In W. Agor (Ed.), *Intuition in Organizations: Leading and Managing Productively*. Newbury Park, CA: Sage, 1989.

Zukav, Gary. *The Seat of the Soul*. New York: Fireside, 1989.

JUNG

Hall, James A. *The Jungian Experience: Analysis and Individuation*. Toronto: Inner City, 1986.

Jung, Carl G. "Answer to Job." New York: Bollingen Foundation, 1958.

*——. *Memories, Dreams and Reflections.* Princeton, NJ: Princeton University Press, 1961.

——. (Ed.) *Man and His Symbols.* London: Aldus Books, 1964.

LEADERSHIP

*Autry, James. *Confessions of an Accidental Businessman.* San Francisco: Berrett-Koehler, 1996.

Carnegie, Dale. *The Power of Positive Thinking.* New York: Prentice-Hall, 1952.

*Chatterjee, Debashis. *Leading Consciously: A Pilgrimage Toward Self Mastery.* Boston: Butterworth-Heinemann, 1998.

*Covey, Stephen. *The Seven Habits of Highly Effective People.* New York: Fireside, 1989.

*Frenier, Carol R. *Business and the Feminine Principle: The Untapped Resource.* Boston, Butterworth-Heinemann, 1997.

*Greenleaf, Robert K. *Servant Leadership: A Journey Into the Nature of Legitimate Power and Greatness.* New York: Paulist, 1977.

*Hill, Napoleon. *Think and Grow Rich.* New York: Fawcett Crest, 1937.

*Hill, Napoleon. *Success through a Positive Mental Attitude.* New York: Pocket Books, 1977.

*Hillman, James. *The Soul's Code: In Search of Character and Calling.* New York: Warner Books, 1996.

Kouzes, James and Barry Posner. *The Leadership Challenge.* San Francisco: Jossey-Bass, 1987.

*Land, George, and Beth Harman. *Breakpoint and Beyond: Mastering the Future—Today.* New York: Harper Business, 1992.

*Lindbergh, Charles. *Autobiography of Values.* New York: Harcourt Brace Jovanovich, 1977.

*Morgenroth, Lynda. "The Making of a Mensch." *Yankee Magazine,* December 1996.

*Senge, Peter. *The Fifth Discipline.* New York: Doubleday, 1990.

Shipka, Barbara. *Leadership in a Challenging World: A Sacred Journey.* Boston: Butterworth-Heinemann, 1997.

*Tracy, B. (Speaker). *The Psychology of Achievement* (Cassette Recording No. 5). Chicago: Nightingale-Conant, 1984.

*Wheatley, Margaret. *Leadership and the New Science: Learning about Organization from an Orderly Universe*. San Francisco: Berrett-Koehler, 1992.

*Wheatley, Margaret and Myron Kellner-Rogers. *A Simpler Way*. San Francisco: Berrett-Koehler, 1996.

*Whyte, David. *The Heart Aroused*. New York: Currency Doubleday, 1994.

*Williams, Terry Tempest. *An Unspoken Hunger*. New York: Vintage Books, 1994.

SCIENCE

*Fuller, Buckminster. *The Critical Path*. New York: St. Martin's Press, 1981.

Lemkov, Anna. *The Wholeness Principle: Dynamics of Unity Within Science, Religion and Society*. Wheaton, IL: The Theosophical Publishing House, 1990.

*Talbot, Michael. *The Holographic Universe*. New York: HarperCollins, 1991.

Wolf, Fred Alan. *Parallel Universes: The Search for Other Worlds*. New York: Touchstone, 1988.

SPIRITUALITY

*Dossey, Larry. *Be Careful What You Pray For: You Just Might Get It*. San Francisco: HarperSanFrancisco: 1997.

Guiley, Rosemary Ellen. *Harper's Encyclopedia of Mystical and Paranormal Experience*. New York: HarperCollins, 1991.

*Hubbard, Barbara Marx. *The Evolutionary Journey: A Personal Guide to a Positive Future*. San Francisco: Evolutionary Press, 1982.

——. *The Revelation: Our Crisis is a Birth*. Novato, CA: Nataraj Publishing, 1993.

Kornfield, Jack. *A Path With Heart: A Guide Through the Perils and Promises of Spiritual Life*. New York: Bantam Books, 1993.

Myss, Caroline. *Anatomy of the Spirit: The Seven Stages of Power and Healing*. New York: Harmony, 1996.

*Palmer, Parker. *To Know as We Are Known*. San Francisco: HarperSan Francisco, 1993.

*Rilke, Rainier Marie. *Letters to a Young Poet*. Boston: Shambala, 1984.

*Sams, Jamie and David Carson. *Medicine Cards*. Santa Fe: Bear & Company, 1998.

*Self-Realization Fellowship. *Inner Reflections Calendar*. Los Angeles: Self-Realization Fellowship, 1997.

Teilhard de Chardin, P. *Activation of Energy*. New York: Harcourt, Brace & Jovanovich. 1970.

*———. *The Phenomenon of Man*. New York: Harper Torchbooks, 1959.

Underhill, Evelyn. *Mysticism: The Preeminent Study in the Nature and Development of Spiritual Consciousness*. New York: Image, 1990.

Yogananda, Paramahansa. *Autobiography of a Yogi*. Los Angeles: Self-Realization Fellowship, 1946, 1990.

VOCATION

Bolles, Richard Nelson. *What Color Is Your Parachute?* Berkeley: Ten Speed Press, 1996.

Sher, Barbara with Annie Gottlieb. *Wishcraft: How to Get What You Really Want*. New York: Ballantine, 1979.

Sinetar, Marsha. *To Build the Life You Want, Create the Work You Love*. New York: St. Martin's Press, 1995.

OTHER

*Breathnach, Sarah Ban. *Simple Abundance*. New York: Warner, 1995.

Castaneda, Carlos. *Journey to Ixtlan: The Lessons of Don Juan*. New York: Washington Square Books, 1973.

Hay, Louise. *You Can Heal Your Life*. Carlsbad, CA: Hay House, 1987.

*Lamott, Anne. *Bird by Bird: Some Instructions on Writing and Life*. New York: Anchor Books, 1994.

*L'Engle, Madeleine. *A Circle of Quiet*. New York: Harper and Row, 1972.

*Matthews, Caitlin. *The Celtic Book of Days*. Rochester, VT: Destiny Books, 1995.

O'Donahue, John. *Anam Cara*. London: Transworld Publishers, 1997.

Tuhy, John E. and Sam Hill. *The Prince of Castle Nowhere*. Portland, OR: Timber Press, 1983.

Webster, N. *Webster's New Twentieth Century Dictionary of the English Language*. 2nd ed. San Francisco: Collins World, 1975.

Index

Butterworth-Heinemann Business Books . . .
for Transforming Business

After Atlantis: Working, Managing, and Leading in Turbulent Times
Ned Hanson, 0-7506-9884-5

The Alchemy of Fear: How to Break the Corporate Trance and Create Your Company's Successful Future
Kay Gilley, 0-7506-9909-4

Beyond Business As Usual: Practical Lessons In Accessing New Dimensions
Michael Munn, 0-7506-9926-4

Beyond Strategic Vision: Effective Corporate Action with Hoshin Planning,
Michael Cowley and Ellen Domb, 0-7506-9843-8

Beyond Time Management: Business with Purpose
Robert A. Wright, 0-7506-9799-7

The Breakdown of Hierarchy: Communicating in the Evolving Workplace
Eugene Marlow and Patricia O'Connor Wilson, 0-7506-9746-6

Business and the Feminine Principle: The Untapped Resource
Carol R. Frenier, 0-7506-9829-2

Business Ecology: Giving Your Organization the Natural Edge
Joseph M. Abe, David A. Bassett, and Patricia E. Demspey, 0-7506-9955-8

Coaching: Evoking Excellence in Others
James Flaherty, 0-7506-9903-5

Choosing the Future: The Power of Strategic Thinking
Stuart Wells, 0-7506-9876-4

Conscious Capitalism: Principles for Prosperity
David A. Schwerin, 0-7506-7021-5

Corporate DNA: Learning from Life
Ken Baskin, 0-7506-9844-6

Cultivating Common Ground: Releasing the Power of Relationships at Work
Daniel S. Hanson, 0-7506-9832-2

Diversity Success Strategies
Norma Carr-Ruffino, 0-7506-7102-5

5th Generation Management, Co-creating Through Virtual Enterprising, Dynamic Teaming, and Knowledge Networking, Revised Edition
Charles M. Savage, 0-7506-9701-6

Flight of the Phoenix: Soaring to Success in the 21st Century
John Whiteside and Sandra Egli, 0-7506-9798-9

From Chaos to Coherence: Advancing Individual and Organizational Intelligence Through Inner Quality Management®
Bruce Cryer and Doc Childre, 0-75067007-X

Getting a Grip on Tomorrow: Your Guide to Survival and Success in the Changed World of Work
Mike Johnson, 0-7506-9758-X

Innovation Strategy for the Knowledge Economy: The Ken Awakening
Debra M. Amidon, 0-7506-9841-1

The Hidden Intelligence: Innovation Through Intuition
Sandra Weintraub, 0-7506-9937-X

The Intelligence Advantage: Organizing for Complexity
Michael D. McMaster, 0-7506-9792-X

The Knowledge Evolution: Expanding Organizational Intelligence
Verna Allee, 0-7506-9842-X

Leadership in a Challenging World: A Sacred Journey
Barbara Shipka, 0-7506-9750-4

Leading Consciously: A Pilgrimage Toward Self-Mastery
Debashis Chatterjee, 0-7506-9864-0

Leading from the Heart: Choosing Courage over Fear in the Workplace
Kay Gilley, 0-7506-9835-7

Learning to Read the Signs: Reclaiming Pragmatism in Business
F. Byron Nahser, 0-7506-9901-9

Leveraging People and Profit: The Hard Work of Soft Management
Bernard A. Nagle and Perry Pascarella, 0-7506-9961-2

Liberating the Corporate Soul: Building A Visionary Organization
Richard Barrett, 0-7506-7071-1

A Little Knowledge Is A Dangerous Thing: Understanding Our Global Knowledge Economy
Dale Neef, 0-7506-7061-4

Marketing Plans that Work: Targeting Growth and Profitability
Malcolm H.B. McDonald and Warren J. Keegan, 0-7506-9828-4

Navigating Cross-Cultural Ethics: What Global Managers Do Right to Keep From Going Wrong
Eileen Morgan, 0-7506-9915-9

A Place to Shine: Emerging from the Shadows at Work
Daniel S. Hanson, 0-7506-9738-5

Power Partnering: A Strategy for Business Excellence in the 21st Century
Sean Gadman, 0-7506-9809-8

Putting Emotional Intelligence to Work; Successful Leadership Is More Than IQ
David Ryback, 0-7506-9956-6

Quantum Leaps: 7 Skills for Workplace ReCreation
Charlotte A. Shelton, 0-7506-7077-0

Resources for the Knowledge-Based Economy Series

> *Knowledge Management and Organizational Design*
> Paul S. Myers, 0-7506-9749-0
>
> *Knowledge Management Tools*
> Rudy L. Ruggles, III, 0-7506-9849-7
>
> *Knowledge in Organizations*
> Laurence Prusak, 0-7506-9718-0
>
> *The Strategic Management of Intellectual Capital*
> David A. Klein, 0-7506-9850-0
>
> *Rise of the Knowledge Worker*
> James W. Cortada, 0-7506-7058-4
>
> *The Knowledge Economy*
> Dale Neef, 0-7506-9936-1
>
> *The Economic Impact of Knowledge*
> Dale Neef, Jacquie Cefola, G. Anthony Seisfeld, 0-7506-7009-6
>
> *Knowledge and Special Libraries*
> James A. Matarazzo and Suzanne D. Connolly, 0-7506-7084-3
>
> Knowledge and Strategy
> Michael Zack, 0-7506-7088-6
>
> Knowledge, Groupware and the Internet
> David Smith, 0-7506-7111-4

To purchase a copy of any Butterworth-Heinemann Business title, please visit your local bookstore or call 1-800-366-2665.

Biography

Dr. Jessika Satori is a Venture Catalyst. She is a creative and successful entrepreneur, consultant, educator, and mentor.

Her ventures include Your Next Step, a personal and career coaching business that specializes in educating and supporting entrepreneurs. For The Record is a records management and archives consulting firm that serves both public and private organizations.

Jessika publishes a newsletter, IntuitionVision that explores the use of intuition in the workplace and in the world. She consults with individuals and organizations about intuitive decision-making. Jessika has given presentations at the Intuition Seminar–at–Sea in the Caribbean.

Dr. Satori assisted futurist and author Barbara Marx Hubbard at the Foundation for Conscious Evolution in San Rafael, California with marketing research and training programs. She was chosen for a State of Washington Governor's Executive Fellowship. She is currently involved in developing educational software programs for Russian entrepreneurs.

Jessika Satori earned her doctorate in Educational Leadership, with studies in Business and Public Administration. She holds an MBA in Entrepreneurship.